Donna:

With Best wishes

Kanwar Prakash Singh

October 17, 2003

Buddhist Temple
Bangkok, Thailand

Trafalgar Square, London

1976

Golden Temple   Amritsar Punjab India

The ART and SPIRIT of
K.P. SINGH

Selected Drawings and Writings

THE ART AND SPIRIT OF K.P. SINGH
by Kanwal Prakash Singh

Copyright © 2003
by Guild Press-Emmis Publishing

ALL RIGHTS RESERVED under
International and Pan-American
Copyright Conventions.

Published in the United States by
GUILD PRESS-EMMIS PUBLISHING, INC.
Indianapolis, Indiana

ISBN 1-57860-120-7
Printed in Mexico

K.P. SINGH

Reflections on Beloved Darjee

His thoughts come to me in the night and at all hours of the day:
As the birds sing their songs of Praise, the temple Shabads fill the predawn
As the flowers open to greet the morning light, the Sun-god blazes across the sky
As the leaves dance in the wind, the falling raindrops glisten in the sun
As the stillness descends upon the landscape, the evening calls the faithful to prayer
As the stars emerge upon the heaven's canopy for their nightly play
As Man and Nature travel through another day of God's wonderful Creation.

Each day, strengthened by new reflections of shared memories
I build loving "monuments" in his honor, relive my past
Celebrate his life, vision, triumphs, and struggles
Enshrine his gifts as prized relics, as cherished legacy,
Embrace his goodness in all its noble simplicity
Invite his blessings, wisdom, and inspirations into my heart,
Capture his warm spirit floating past my mind's "window"
Add a splash of living color and purpose to my unfinished passage
In hopes to walk beyond tomorrows into Eternity, hand in hand.

His ways were beloved; a rare gentleness guided his life
He radiated wisdom of old souls, scattered kindly light all around
His boundless spirit left delicate imprints all over mine.
Humble beginnings, the Partition, and uncertainties tested his grace
He was too busy to despair over the unwelcome and unsettling disruptions
Often choosing challenge, faith, sacrifice, hope as his cherished friends.

He triumphed over trivia, nearly overcame the worldly distractions
Found his strength in Hukam, Simran, Seva: surrender, meditation, service
Tirelessly striving to dispel darkness within, illumine his spirit with loving Light.
He gravitated to "centers" of true learning searching for lasting gifts:

Discipline, character, compassion, freedom from ignorance, envy, and pride.
He enshrined the noblest inspirations and toiled to give them shape
He taught others to explore their own daring dreams.

Admirers showered affection upon this enlightened teacher
Welcomed as he walked across the thresholds of life.
With a radiant smile, with his head held high
He surrendered his all in service and thanksgiving.
His "cycles of separation" ended, his soul merged with the Universal Soul,
His light mingled with the Eternal Light of Ages.
I imagine, he resides somewhere among the stars, amidst the very blessed
His modest brilliance now part of the dazzling splendor of the Heavens.

I am fortunate to call this wonderful mentor my own;
He shaped my life and gave birth to my dreams.
Dare I imitate the trail he blazed, the life he lived?
Can I risk in my ignorance to intrude upon his noble legacy,
Trespass across the uncommon thresholds of his exemplary life?
Can a candle stand up to the sun?

No, I shall not imitate, nor pretend to be in his image.
I must follow my own star, discover my own trail
Wander the seashore in search of new gems from the deep
Weave the uncommon legacy of his life into my own.
Then ask God: mend my broken threads, unite the separated hearts
Keep Thy Living Presence, Thy boundless Love all around
Guide my labors that in gratitude and loving memory
Build new "monuments" that honor and celebrate Life.

DEDICATION

I dedicate this book to my beloved darjee (father), Jogindar Singh,
a scholar, an enlightened teacher, and a noble spirit.
He continues to be a guiding light in my life.

CONTENTS

FOREWORD

K.P. Singh and I made independent decisions to serve the people of Indianapolis, Indiana, in 1967. As a native of Indianapolis with five generations of Hoosier roots, I had returned from naval service in 1960, helped manage family businesses, served on the school board, and ran successfully for mayor in 1967. K.P.'s family had fled Pakistan and settled safe but penniless in India in 1947 in the midst of partition of the country and violence that claimed as many as a million lives. Two decades later, in 1967, he came to Indianapolis as a senior urban planner in the Department of Metropolitan Development after completing graduate studies at the University of Michigan. He had lived in the United States for only two years. During that time he had experienced ignorance of the Sikh faith and even some hostility in Detroit and then Indianapolis.

I do not remember the day we met, but we were destined to find each other in the City-County Building and in the neighborhoods of Indianapolis. Our city was in the midst of the civil rights revolution of the late 1960's. As mayor, I was attempting to enlist citizens of all faiths, races, and creeds to hold the city together even as many other large northern cities suffered disorder, destruction, and death. My dream was to bring political unity to the inner-city and suburbs and use that stronger foundation to appeal to the world to invest talent and money in our city.

The future of Indianapolis was always on K.P. Singh's drawing board, but as an urban planner at the heart of the unified government in our city, he was excited not only by what could be built in the future, but also by the beauty of the city's abundant and under-appreciated historic architecture. He ignored the thoughtless comments of those who misunderstood his turban or other aspects of superficial appearance and calmly told new Hoosier friends that they were surrounded by a rich legacy of remarkable buildings that expressed and perpetuated our deepest feelings of love and faith. He introduced me to an Indian festival and to the Indian community in Indianapolis. K.P. dreamed that his new friends in Indiana would discover the rest of the world and that the world would reciprocate that enthusiasm.

When President Richard Nixon came to Indianapolis at the beginning of 1970, he asked Daniel Patrick Moynihan and me to represent the United States at the NATO Conference on the Challenges of Modern Society in Brussels, Belgium. Stimulated by this conference, I subsequently invited mayors, urban planners, and champions of cities from all over the world to come to Indianapolis for a Conference on Cities in 1971. A 500-voice high school chorus sang "Ode to Joy" on the Monument Circle to greet our guests from abroad. Local ethnic groups organized dinners for foreign nationals now united with kindred spirits in our city. K.P. was active in the planning for this ambitious event, but he became even more energized when it appeared that Union Station, the historic shrine of railroad operations in Indianapolis, might be in jeopardy. He found that many other citizens shared his concern, including the mayor, but few could articulate the spirit and the beauty of Union Station better than he could. He founded K.P. Singh Designs in 1972 and began a remarkable advocacy for historic buildings in Indianapolis and throughout the world, through pen-and-ink drawings.

Thirty years later, the scope of his work is astonishing. In this book, *The Art and Spirit of K.P. Singh*, we are introduced to 200 of his most important drawings from around the world and many of his most compelling thoughts about how he has manifested faith, spirit, beauty, and historical heritage through his art.

K.P. has presented prints of many of his drawings to me, and I cherish each one in an honored place in my office or my home. In my Hart Senate Office Building Conference Room, where I have received many heads of state and other distinguished guests each year, I have hung "Cathedrals of the Spirit" from the K.P. Singh 25th Year Retrospective Exhibit, "President Benjamin Harrison's House," "The Columbia Club," and "Hendricks County, Indiana" a print of the work that Hendricks County Commissioners presented to former President Ronald Reagan during his presidential visit to Danville in 1987.

During the years that I have served as a member and chairman of the Senate Foreign Relations Committee, K.P. has shared with me his thoughts about India and Pakistan and his views on a host of foreign policy dilemmas. He travels widely, and he is deeply sensitive to human suffering, which he witnessed as a seven-year-old boy in 1947 and far too often ever since. But his outlook is always one of optimism and reverence for all that he finds beautiful and then shares with us through his drawings. He is a loving and devoted husband and father and a man I have been proud to call a loyal friend.

This beautiful book reminds me of the many ways that we have journeyed together since 1967, of how much our comprehension of the world has grown, and of how much we hope to do in the years ahead. *The Art and Spirit of K.P. Singh* is a celebration of beautiful creative spaces in which faith and wisdom may grow and a stimulus to all of us to give thanks to our Creator for life and for so many wonderful opportunities.

RICHARD G. LUGAR
United States Senator
Indiana
December 31, 2002

INTRODUCTION

LETTER AND SPIRIT

These selected drawings of historic buildings, landmark monuments, sacred sites, college campuses, and community attractions are from many places around the world. In spotlighting architectural landmarks and other historically significant sites, I hope that responsible steps will be taken to ensure their continuity and rightful heritage in our communities. Civic leaders and the public must consider preservation, restoration, and adaptation to new uses as important options to losing them to contemporary community pressures and unconscionable neglect.

This book is also about my writings: musings on matters of spirit. Drawing from my own experiences and beliefs that form the foundations of my life, I am sharing personal, philosophical, and spiritual reflections. It is not my intention to infringe on any one's sacred rights, cultural sensitivities, or personal dignity. I proclaim no superiority for my points of view. For me, all diverse ideas and cherished ideals deserve respect. It is my modest hope that these thoughts and images may echo in the lives and experiences of many, and they may discover inspirations in this book.

This book is not about history, art, or geograph, nor is this an autobiography. This book is about the many universal thoughts and images. This book is about appreciating and enjoying our architectural and artistic legacy that provide an understanding of our journey as a civilization. For me, all matters relating to life, various art forms, and culture are extensions and mirrors of our spirit. Our unique perspectives might vary, but we are looking toward the same horizons of hope, dreams, and promise of life.

ARCHITECTURE: A CANOPY FOR LIFE AND SPIRIT

Architecture is a great source for learning, ecstasy, and indescribable wonder. Architecture offers reflections of ethnic, cultural, and spiritual journeys, as well as the influence of history, geography, and time. Magnificent space and enclosures, created and embellished with a wide variety of building materials and design treatments, provide a measure of artistic achievements, adaptations, and innovations. Architecture is an expression of human imagination and creativity. In architecture, the world of art, culture, and the spirit complement and ornament each other, dancing in harmony.

SPIRIT: A UNIVERSAL CENTRAL PILLAR OF LIFE

I understand our spirit as the central pillar of Life. It is an anchor of faith, vision, and promise, the very essence of our humanity. We share this precious blessing with all living beings. Spirit is an invisible life-force that defines who we are and what we can be. It threads and transcends all areas of human endeavor. Spirit provides direction to our hopes, dreams, and spiritual energy to our creative urges. Spirit needs and seeks a pleasant, uplifting, and healthy environment to prosper. This has led to the art of creating defined spaces and building special enclosures for various human activities.

HUMAN SPIRIT: A TRUE REFLECTION AND COMPOSITE OF LIFE

The spirit, as a colorful and powerful component of our humanity, is much more than what its simple definition might suggest. It is a repository of our emotions, reflections, and responses to the promise and functions of Life. Our spirit may carry recollections and memories of lives and times past. Each spirit has its own unique code that guides our individual and collective response and shapes our cultural and spiritual rhythms. The spirit, as a deeply enshrined source of our being, carries its own special vibrancy and personality. Our spirit, as a witness to life, can offer a window to our soul.

IN SEARCH OF LIGHT

Like many, I am in search of the meaning and purpose of life. My thoughts often gravitate towards people who exude Light and optimism, radiate goodness, and friendliness. My heart is caught in the magic of sensual attachments and attractions. My mind yearns to travel in spirit with the great souls who exhibit a zest for life and Seva (selfless service), blaze new trails, discover new frontiers, and display courage to embrace the unfamiliar. For me, their lives and spirits are a tribute to the Divine.

I have learned much from the exemplary lives of such enlightened teachers. I marvel at their spirit that knows or recognizes no bounds. Such souls reject all narrow perspectives that divide people. They always live in the Light, tirelessly strive and sacrifice to unite and honor our common and cherished interests. They remind us that the spirit that dwells in darkness, pessimism, and selfish pursuits has little to spare to uplift others. They represent triumphs and sacred energy that have given man some of our most cherished gifts. My writings reflect my deep gratitude for their inspirations.

WEAVING IMAGES WITH WORDS

My writings focus on my encounters and reflections that bring hope, healing, and creative inspirations and that uplift my heart and spirit. I derive my inspiration from the unfathomable mystery and magnificence of Creation revealed in the Sikh and other scriptures and works of distinguished poets and scholars.

I have tried to capture and express in words some universal ideas. My distinct linguistic, ethnic, cultural, and faith foundation is woven into my writings. A spectacle of images, native sounds, maddening noises, mysterious auras, and imprints of my Punjabi (mother tongue and cultural origin), often float across my mind's landscapes like glistening clouds. Fleeting images of my past compete with new ideas to trace and shape new cultural scripts over the old. Transliteration of the true essence of my life-scripts into the English language presented its own challenge.

There is not much new under the literary heavens about matters of spirit. Someone has already said it much more beautifully. My modest attempt at writing breaks no new ground. I share my experiences, insights, inspirations, and perspectives. I have much to learn. I pray for your indulgence.

OTHER INSPIRATIONS AND MENTORS

My family, childhood experiences, and life journey have had a profound impact on me. My mind often travels back to my childhood and our miraculous escape from death when I remember the nightmare in the wake of the 1947 Partition of India. We witnessed unimagined tragedy and the forced transfer of populations (we call it ethnic cleansing today). I remember the uncertainty, the caravans of terrified displaced humanity, my family's flight to safety into India, and the struggles that followed. Our ancestral homes and my place of birth are now a part of a newly created Pakistan. This has left permanent imprints on my body, mind, and soul.

God's guiding hand led us forward. I recollect with pride my educational pursuits in India, my arrival in the USA for higher studies in 1965, and settling in Indiana in 1967 to build a future. Each "visit" to my past inspires new lessons and an appreciation of my greatest blessings.

My father has enriched my ideas and spirit beyond measure. He was an enlightened teacher, a scholar of languages, and an author. He set a wonderful example for his seven children. His simple life, courage, and humanity continue to be my guiding light and a cherished presence in my journey. My mother was a saint and symbolized all that is good about humanity. Family in India and many friends in the USA have provided me boundless love. My wife and children have helped me to shed the stubborn emotional burdens of yesterday and embrace new focus and excitement for tomorrow.

EMBRACING THE CIRCLE OF LIGHT

My early childhood experiences deepened my interest in matters of spirit. I believe that each faith tradition and spiritual inspiration enhances the Circle of Light. Understanding and appreciating the full spectrum of cultural and spiritual tapestry around us can greatly enhance our own spirit. This realization has given me new perspectives and insights about life, faith, service, spirituality, and sense of community.

Being mindful of my blessings and mortality keeps me grounded. I understand that life is a precious gift and that "Every living being is a repository of Divine Light." The Sikh scriptures further reveal and affirm that "we are placed on this Earth to know God, serve others, and show understanding and compassion toward all." My writings are my prayers, meditations, hopes, my songs and yearnings to connect with my deeper self. They are my search for the "Divine within" and the Divine all around.

Readers will find meaning in ideas that reflect their convictions and spirit, but I hope that my writings offer a different cultural, ethnic, and spiritual perspective that may resonate with many. We are all unique. We all dance to our own inner stirrings, and yet we share many universal precepts, hopes, inspirations, dreams, and struggles. I extend a gentle reminder and challenge: let us discover and strengthen these common threads and know our own true spirit.

SPIRIT IN ARCHITECTURE

Beyond the apparent diversity of cultural and spiritual geography, we can witness that the architecture for living, working, worship, celebration, and recreation include some elements that demonstrate our common needs, expectations, and visions. We seek safety and comfort in our living environment. We expect grandeur, opulence, and symbolism in the landmarks of authority and buildings of community and national significance. In sacred architecture, we strive for artistic excellence and an environment that uplifts the spirit and inspires devotion.

In sacred architecture, we have brilliantly transposed the temporal functions with our concepts of celestial beauty and majestic splendor. Architectural styles, designs, building materials, and treatments greatly vary. The results at times have been spectacular, as evident in the grand "Cathedrals of Spirit" of major faith traditions. There have been some endeavors of unsurpassed architectural, artistic, and spiritual achievements.

Architecture for work has often followed the concepts of economy, practicality, stimulation, productivity, and corporate identity. Our commercial landmarks often incorporate designs and features that make statements of distinction. There is a fierce competition among corporations to establish a dominant presence in our metropolitan cityscapes and skylines. The ultimate goal is to grow in economic power.

Educational institutions skillfully combine the environment for learning, unique history, spirit, and tradition of the school. With the new fields of learning arrived demands for continued expansion of facilities. Today, campus architecture often features a composite of many architectural styles that emerged during the various periods of its growth. Landmarks, attractions, and other special elements that enhance the school spirit, image, and standing among rival institutions are carefully integrated into campus life and design.

The county courthouses: "Temples of Justice" often adopted imposing styles that proclaimed authority and announced their special status in the community. The American "Courthouse Square" provided the backdrop and the front seat for many important events in our history. They continue to be a major attraction even today. In courthouse architecture, various building styles, design motifs, and many artistic and cultural influences combine to reveal the national origins, spirit, and legacy of the early settlers.

ARCHITECTURE IN SETTINGS

Throughout history, the builders sought settings that added distinction, drama, and beauty to architecture: lakes, rivers, ocean-fronts, mountain tops, unusual landscapes, ancient sites and settlements, and urban skylines. We witness attention to detail: imaginative natural and man-made surroundings, attractive views and vista, breath-taking transitional spaces, and richly embellished interior spaces and exterior facades.

To maximize impact and aesthetics, the builders used a rich composite of natural elements and artistic creations. They incorporated fountains, reflecting pools, statues, formal gardens and rich landscape, beautiful doorways, paintings and murals, inlay-work, patterns, stained-glass windows, skylights, majestic gilded domes, magnificent vaulted ceilings, and other features that proclaim cultural identity. The builders employed unusual treatments, spatial designs, and materials to fire our imagination and emotions. We witness their spirit in the great works that have survived the ravages of time. These masterpieces and treasures adorn our world with beauty. We must preserve their precious legacy.

The mission to awe and transport the human spirit to a higher realm is central to all religious architecture: from the charming dignity of the modest one-room country church to the ancient temples, mosques, synagogues, and medieval Gothic cathedrals. The fundamental goal is to connect the temporal and mundane elements of our being with the celestial mystery. The design, aesthetics, and the aura of the space speak to us. The images and embellishments have a language of their own. The rich artistic details- icons, motifs, colorful and festive interpretations- help us visualize and imagine unfathomable wonders. Sometimes, the Divine itself seems captured and reflected in our temporal creative manifestations.

Over the centuries, architectural forms and functions have undergone transition. The grandeur of yesterday has been replaced with stark and contemporary boxes of glass and concrete, the extremes of opulence of the past with simplified practicality and efficiency. An expanding global culture and new discoveries continue to bring changes to the arts and the concepts of living, working, worship, and celebration.

MESSAGE WITH LINES

The drawings in this book offer a few examples of the variety of architecture from many places and diverse cultures. We can see changes in architecture brought by time and outside influences. Cultures and people have crossed old traditional boundaries. It is evident that new immigrants, to affirm their link with the past, have adapted familiar architectural styles and artistic treatments from native countries to their new environment. Sometimes, many influences seem to overlap in the same structure, heralding the emergence of new architectural styles and building trends in our communities.

Through my art, I rediscover a small fragment of our architectural past. Art is my medium to communicate and educate others about the importance of historic architecture and draw attention to this resource. In recent decades, we have lost many architectural gems to destruction, environment, economic pressures, and urban sprawl. In communities across the globe, devastating short-sighted planning policies have taken their toll on our architectural heritage.

My drawings are a tribute to the history, art, and spirit of architecture. The integrated script in some of the composite drawings highlights elements of their significance. My drawings are an invitation to enjoy, explore, and discover special treasures in our own communities. Efforts to preserve them may follow.

If lines on paper could speak, they would reveal that our heritage is an extension of our spirit. These images invite us to imagine buildings as "living entities" and transport our spirit to another time and place. They highlight visual details that we can only see if we were approaching them as pedestrians. The drawings may stimulate interest and appreciation of the architecture around us. Architecture, as a witness to history, introduces us to the life, spirit, and genius of early pioneers. My drawings, besides their intrinsic value as objects of art to enjoy, are intended to elevate awareness and generate excitement about the contribution that these landmarks make to our environment.

My drawings are a visual introduction to some of the significant and historic real estate in our communities. Preservation on paper does not offer us a full experience: the sights and sounds, the textures and treatments, the emotions and inspirations that being around them alone might inspire. The pen-and-ink linear drawings, with occasional sprinkling of color and script, offer a very limited perspective of the true richness of our cherished architectural heritage. The drawings provide a visual "encounter" with a few gems in the diverse spectrum of our urban tapestries.

Awareness and education alone can assure the continuation of our link with these symbols and icons of our past. Once we recognize their true importance, we may move into action preserving and integrating them into the future fabric of our towns and cities as major cultural and visual anchors. We owe future generations knowledge of our footprints on the landscape of time. They must understand our struggles and journey and inherit this important architectural "trust" from us. By knowing our legacy, creativity, and spirit, they too may be inspired to add their own signature to future survival of our historic architecture.

ABOUT WORDS AND IMAGES

The book has nine broad sections. The drawings and images in each section focus on a distinct category: places of worship, courthouses, colleges, homes, historic monuments, and heritage sites. The text reinforces the letter and spirit of the book. It may not always relate to the section heading or the images that accompany it. The essay theme may continue over several pages. The text covers ideas and reflections on faith, prayer, hope, life, music, art, architecture, and heritage. The writings offer a tribute to human spirit, creativity, and adventure. The thoughts, essays, and poems celebrate life in all its incredible richness and diversity. It is my prayerful hope that the perspectives and reflections offered may enhance our own understanding about the matters of spirit. The architectural drawings, images, and photographs may make each of us more aware of the special heritage and artistic treasures in our own communities and cultures. I am proud to take you on my journey through these drawings and writings.

ANCIENT TEMPLE,
PUSHKAR

Rajasthan, India

CORRIDORS *of* HISTORY

SCATTERED ACROSS THE HUMAN landscape from communities to countries are places that are witness to outstanding events in history. The physical size, style, geography, and archeology of these places and sites varies from a single architectural fragment or building to an entire country, from a single event to a series of events over many centuries. These architectural and cultural corridors may display visible marks of events past or historic records, memorials and monuments, and other visual reminders that transfer this history to succeeding generations.

Invading armies often left devastation along the routes of their march through countries. A large stretch of North India faced countless armies of invaders that came through the famous gateway of the Khyber Pass. If only walls could talk, they would fill our souls with grief and our hearts with great pride. A thousand other cities and sites bear the scars of invasions, desecration, and

Construction of the historic Charles Bridge over the Vltava River in the "Golden Prague" (also known as "The City of One Hundred Towers and Spires") began in 1357 under King Charles IV. Embellished with thirty imposing sculptures and Gothic towers, this Bridge is a major cultural and architectural landmark in the fascinating city of Prague.

Charles Bridge
Prague, Czechoslovakia

Kanwar Prakash Singh
© 2003

CHARLES BRIDGE *Prague, Czechoslovakia*

destruction. Foreign occupation introduced new ideas, cultures, and architectural influences, intruding on the existing order.

Today, there are visible signs of historic battles won and lost on the designs and facades of structures. Many such places are crossroads of culture, trade, and pilgrimages to the past. One can witness the convergence of many architectural and artistic influences at these sites and along these corridors. These places in their original or rebuilt state offer a glimpse of the times, events, spirit, and symbols of defiance and triumph, and connect us with the human journey through the ages.

The selected drawings in this section represent a few architectural and heritage sites that have been witness to invasions, cultural intrusions, and sometimes new and interesting introductions of architectural styles and artistic expressions. The accompanying text relates to personal perspectives and inspirations.

A Living Witness

Architecture is often a "living" witness to culture and history. The beautiful building in a grand setting, a mighty fortress on a lonely landscape, the sacred shrines amidst the cathedrals of nature, and architectural ruins of past grandeur, even in their silence, all offer a living testimony of our civilization. Time and history have left imprints of passage on the architectural heritage that we cherish today.

Architecture commands greater attention and attains special significance when it is intimately associated with the life and times of major historic or religious figures or other landmark events. Architecture becomes a major attraction when it offers an outstanding example and high achievement in the art and science of building.

Geography, cultural traditions, and the state of arts influence the building design and ornamentation. Technology and function may also define the finished edifice. It is a visual transcript of the strengths, struggles, and survival of people and cultures. Celebrated

ST. MARY'S CHURCH *Indianapolis, Indiana*

architecture successfully captures and expresses the true spirit of a building in an attractive form and as an imaginative physical space.

Sacred architecture places greater demands upon the designer, artist, and the builder. Historic and spiritual significance then may play a role in design, form, and aesthetics. In addition, the commands and whims of patrons and powerful religious institutions often influence the final designs. We can only imagine the agony and ecstasy of Michelangelo as the designer of the awesome dome of St. Peter's in Rome and the painter of the Sistine Chapel in the Vatican.

In sacred places and sites, we see deep connections and special significance for our lives and faith: as emotional anchor, spiritual heritage, and faith legacy. Through them, we may recall and relive the significant chapters and major cultural encounters of our faith. We draw strength when we learn about the struggles and sacrifice of the leaders of the faith. We seek renewal and affirmations from

THE CHURCH OF THE ANNUNCIATION - NAZARETH

THE CHURCH OF ST. MARY MAGDALENE

THE DOME OF THE ROCK

THE PLAZA OF THE WAILING WALL / THE WESTERN WALL

MOUNT OF THE BEATITUDES - SEA OF GALILEE

THE CITADEL - JERUSALEM

THE CHURCH OF THE NATIVITY - BETHLEHEM

CHURCH OF THE HOLY SEPULCHRE

THE HILLTOP FORT OF MASADA IN THE DEAD SEA AREA

GREEK MONASTERY OF ST. GEORGE AT WADI KELT

BEIT SHEAN - THE ROMAN THEATRE

THE CHURCH OF ALL NATIONS

HOLOCAUST YAD VASHEM" MEMORIAL

OLD OLIVE TREE IN THE GARDEN OF GETHSEMANE

THE SHRINE OF THE BOOK AND THE KNESSET PARLIAMENT BLDG.

Federation - Maurer Israel Civic Mission V
of the
Jewish Community Relations Council
February 13 - 24 , 1995

Kanwal Prakash Singh
© April 1993

KIBBUTZ KFAR BLUM

THE RIVER JORDAN

BAR MITZVAH CELEBRATION AT THE WESTERN WALL

HISTORIC AND SACRED HERITAGE, ISRAEL

our pilgrimages to such holy sites. The builders were aware of this challenge: to fill the imagination and spirit of the faithful, and the visitor, with wonder, awe, and inspiration.

Once inside, our sight and spirit may encounter sacred icons, magnificent tapestries, paintings and sculpture, breathtaking windows, the dance of light and interior space, colorful mosaics and motifs, and other unusual and unique ornamentation. Intended to inspire images and reflections of the unseen wonder and mystery, sacred places capture visions beyond the material and temporal creations.

Royal brocaded canopies, colorful banners, crystal chandeliers, oriental carpets, and floral decorations often enhance the aura of these places. Music, message, tradition, pageantry, and ceremonies unite to strengthen our faith.

Our sacred shrines are sanctuaries of blissful tranquility amidst an environment of earthly temptations and struggles. The houses of worship offer us a glimpse of the celestial splendor beyond our earthly journey. Each faith may feature architectural and design elements that best reflect its unique tradition, beliefs, and heritage. Each faith may highlight concepts that invite devotion, stimulate our senses, and provide understanding about faith, life, and our place in the universe. Visuals are powerful stimuli to educate and inspire the human mind and spirit.

To achieve such lofty ideals, man has spared no effort or sacrifice. Man has created some of the most beautiful and imaginative structures on the face of the Earth. These architectural wonders inspire awe, deep emotions, reverence, and admiration.

Throughout history, man has made new discoveries, set new sights, and excelled in the art of building. One can witness the hand of angels in some awesome creations: the Gothic cathedrals of Europe; the Golden Temple of the Sikhs at Amritsar, India; the Blue Mosque in Istanbul, Turkey; the Taj Mahal at Agra, India. Ancient Hindu temples of Ajanta Caves, India, the

Covered Bridge - 1856
Parke County, Indiana

Kanwal Prakash Singh
© August 1988

COVERED BRIDGE *Parke County, Indiana*

Great Wall of China, the modern skyscraper, and the many treasures in the cities of Venice, Florence, Jerusalem, and Prague all offer testimony to the marvels of human imagination and spirit.

Man adapted as the civilization spread, exchanging and discovering new architectural styles and making changes to the art of building. Such transitions were not always peaceful, welcome, or easily embraced. Religious and cultural revolts, fanaticism and intolerant rulers, and external invasions left unmistakable evidence and visible scars. Architecture struggled for survival under hostile onslaughts. "Sacrilege" and outrage against artistic and cultural treasures remains etched in the human experience. Destruction and neglect have robbed us of many great treasures. The record of our past architectural and artistic triumphs is incomplete. The surviving buildings, ruins, and fragments provide us a limited "window" to our past journey. This valuable resource and heritage must be preserved for future generations.

Today the human spirit is at the crossroads of an emerging global culture. Ethnic, cultural, and faith boundaries that once separated us are being bridged. Architectural styles and influences are being shared and adapted. Steps are underway to integrate these priceless treasures into the urban, community, and international cultural fabric. As symbols of human creativity and spirit, our architecture reveals much about our civilization's past and future. In an era of expanding global culture, our architecture can become a force for greater good than we could have imagined.

Located 85 Km Northeast of Beirut, towering above the Beqaa plain, Baalbeck is Lebanon's greatest Greco-Roman treasure. Baalbeck Temples: the gigantic Acropolis was built between the 1st and 3rd centuries on the site of an ancient Phoenician temple dedicated to the worship of Baal, a semitic deity. The Romans adopted the Greek name, Heliopolis (city of sun) and dedicated the new temples to Jupiter, Bacchus and Venus. Baalbeck also has other Moslem sites including the Grand Mosque built by Omayyed Caliphs.

Baalbeck, Lebanon   Kanwar-Prakash Singh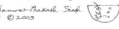
                                     © 2003

BAALBECK, LEBANON

CAPITOL HILL. "THROUGH THE HALLS OF THIS MAGNIFICENT STRUCTURE HAVE PASSED THE LEADING FIGURES IN AMERICAN HISTORY — THE ELECTED REP-
RESENTATIVES OF THE PEOPLE. CONSTRUCTION OF THE U.S. CAPITOL BEGAN IN 1793. PRESIDENT JOHN ADAMS ADDRESSED THE FIRST JOINT
SESSION OF CONGRESS IN THE SENATE CHAMBER ON NOVEMBER 22, 1800, BUT THE BUILDING WAS NOT FINISHED UNTIL 1867."

The U.S. Capitol
Washington D.C.

Ranwar P. Singh
January 20, 1981

THE US CAPITOL *Washington, D.C.*

View of Soldiers and Sailors Monument
Indianapolis, Indiana

Kanwar Prakash Singh
© march 1992

SOLDIERS AND SAILORS MONUMENT *Indianapolis, Indiana*

OLD HOLY CROSS MONASTERY - 1899
CHAPEL - 1895 STYLE : ROMASEQUE
RENAISSAGE

ISSAC M. WISE TEMPLE - 1845
ARCHITECT : JAMES KEYS WILSON

FOUNTAIN SQUARE
TYLER DAVIDSON FOUNTAIN PRESENTED TO
THE CITY OF CINCINNATI BY HENRY PROBASCO IN 1871

CATHEDRAL OF
ST. PETER IN CHAINS - 1845
STYLE · MODIFIED GREEK TEMPLE

CITY HALL - 1893
STYLE · RICHARDSONIAN
ROMANESQUE
ARCHITECT : SAMUEL HANNAFORD

CINCINNATI ART MUSEUM - 1866
ARCHITECT : JAMES McLAUGHIN

SUSPENSION BRIDGE (OVER OHIO RIVER) - 1867
DESIGNED BY : JOHN ROEBLING

RIVER-FRONT SPORTS STADIUM - 1970
(CINCINNATI SKYLINE IN THE BACKGROUND)

OHIO'S FIRST PRESIDENT

GENERAL WILLIAM HENRY HARRISON

CINCINNATI SKYLINE FROM KENTUCKY SIDE OF OHIO RIVER

OLD CINCINNATI UNION TERMINAL - 1933 MURALS BY : WINOLD REISS
STYLE : ART-DECO   (MOSAIC TILES)
ARCHITECTS : ALFRED FELLHEIMER
STEWART WAGNER

525 VINE STREET BLDG.
ARCHITECTS : GLASER & ASSOC.
1984

THE FOUNDING OF CITY OF CINCINNATI (ORIGINALLY KNOWN AS LOSANTIVILLE) DATES BACK TO 1788. BORDERED BY
OHIO RIVER AND CROWNED BY LUSH GREEN HILLS AND BECAUSE OF ITS MANY SCENIC ATTRACTIONS AS WELL AS HISTORIC AND CULTURAL INTERESTS,
CINCINNATI BECAME THE LARGEST AND THE FASTEST GROWING METROPOLIS WEST OF THE ALLEGHENIES BY MID-19TH CENTURY. BECAUSE OF ITS SETTING AND BEAUTY, IT BECAME KNOWN AS
"THE QUEEN CITY OF THE WEST." SIR WINSTON CHURCHILL CALLED CINCINNATI "THE MOST BEAUTIFUL INLAND CITY IN AMERICA". CINCINNATI PROMISES NO LESS IN THE FUTURE . IT IS A CITY ON THE MOVE.

Cincinnati : The Queen City , Ohio , U.S.A.

Kanwal Prakash Singh
September 1987

THE QUEEN CITY *Cincinnati, Ohio*

Time and Life

UNION STATION *Indianapolis, Indiana*

The inseparable companions move forward, often in mysterious ways.
Time, in mystical obedience, designated cycles, measured rhythms,
Life, in untamed mystery, surprising leaps, unexpected jolts
Taking our destiny through unknown valleys and unimagined crossings.

Life moves forward.
Time must march on and does.
No one can stop the hands of Time
Nor fully comprehend the mysterious rhythms of Life.

Time assures change.
Life promises unpredictable encounters, daily new lessons,
Each directed to open our mind to the unseen and the possible.
Lead our spirit in the destined paths for our lives.

Life may serve uncertainty or cherished rewards
Reflecting the imprints of our Karma from another lifetime,
Revealing the ordained Will for our life this time around.
Guide our spirit past struggles, in new directions, undreamed of horizons.

Welcome, explore the promise in each new experience;
Gather, enshrine the rich offerings along the colorful seashore of Life.

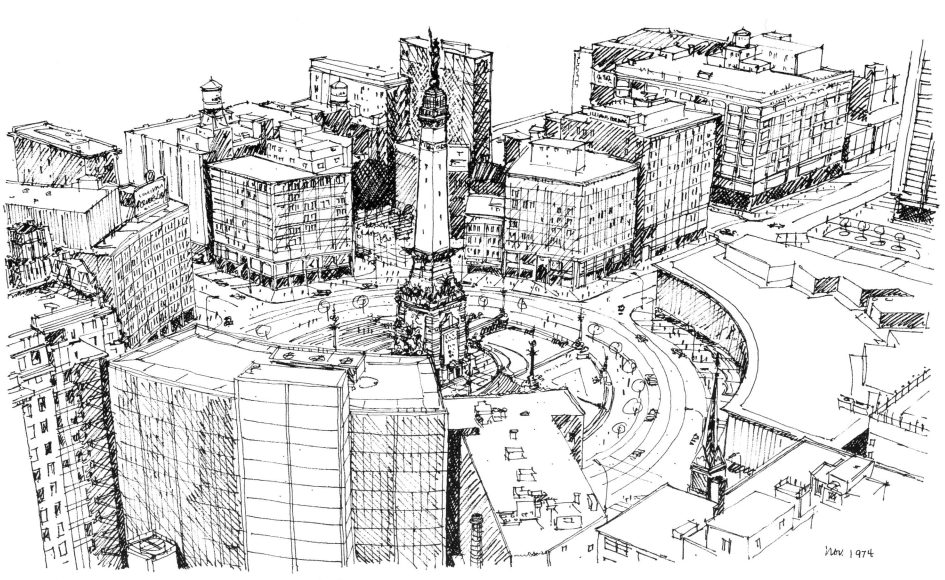

Nov. 1974

The Soldiers and Sailors monument completed in 1902
rises majestically to a height of 184 feet in the very heart
of the City of Indianapolis. The Monument and the
surrounding buildings create a very interesting urban
space.

Monument Circle II

Banwal Prakash Singh

MONUMENT CIRCLE *Indianapolis, Indiana*

MISSION DELORES *San Francisco, California*

Share a generous measure of Light and Hope with others in search of their destiny.
With Seva and Simran as anchor, discover the true promise of our own lifetime.

Meditation:

May our life be guided by wisdom, not wants,
Thoughts, pursuits, and learning that steady our spirit,
Faith and spirit that recognize the Divine Hand in all things.

Inspirations and insights that witness the blessed marvel all around;
Heart and hands serve and fashion special gifts for the Altar of Life;
Patience and strength lead past the daily trials, darkness, magic and surprise;
Knowing and understanding: God shall reveal the guarded mystery of Life in Time.

OLD NORTH CHURCH:
Built in 1723, it is Boston's
oldest standing church.

BOSTON:
Boston has held a place of special
honor in American history since
the colonial days. It has been
called the "Birthplace of
American Freedom" for their role in the
War of Independence.
Contemporary Boston has preserved a number of
Revolutionary shrines
including those of such great
men as John Adams, John Hancock,
and Paul Revere, whose words and
deeds serve as an inspiration as the
nation celebrates its Bicentennial.

PAUL REVERE

BOSTON CITY HALL

PAUL REVERE MALL:
The statue by Cyrus Dallin.
13 Bronze tablets set in
the surrounding wall
describe the part played
by the North End people
in Boston's history from
1630 to 1918.

FANEUIL HALL: Also called "The Cradle of Liberty",
it was given to the people of Boston by merchant
Peter Faneuil in 1742.

Boston   Massachusetts

Leanward P. Singh
December 1975

My Family's Flight

I often reflect on God's continued reassurance, compassion, and faith in us. Miracles of destiny unfold in the midst of hopelessness and uncertainty, and we personally witness God's boundless love.

The sacred texts and traditions of all faiths enshrine testimony of divine intervention. Sikh scriptures affirm, "When God's grace is upon us, undreamed of blessings are showered upon us." God guides us across the "vast ocean of temporal suffering." The all-knowing, "forgiving and compassionate Lord ignores our inequities and comforts us in our hour of sorrow and suffering" and "breathes new life after taking away life." God carries us from the valley of darkness, doubt, and mortal danger to safety and sunshine.

More than half a century ago, sensing danger, our family handed the keys of our ancestral home to a Muslim friend and decided to flee to safety. My hometown, Jaranwala, in the former Punjab Province of India, was now part of the newly created country of Pakistan. British rule and occupation ended on Aug. 15, 1947, with the partition of India.

Based on religious considerations, the partition of India set in motion massive dislocation of populations on both sides of the newly created borders. The declaration of Indian independence turned the simmering conflicts into widespread violence and exodus. Over a million Sikhs, Hindus, and Muslims lost their lives.

Some 20,000 innocent people were massacred in Jaranwala on Sept. 8, 1947. Savagery ravaged the peaceful town that day. Years of communal harmony, shared traditions, and much-heralded spiritual and cultural diversity were shattered.

Our family survived that fateful night and several threatening encounters during our flight to India. We found refuge in prayer, hope, and each other.

I remember being on the sidewalk in Amritsar, an Indian border town, tired, hungry, and disoriented. We feared the fate of other family members. All around us, hordes of dazed refugees agonized about what to do next.

Suddenly a miracle! A search party found us and reunited us with family members who had arrived earlier. Later, when we had lost all hope, our father, grandfather, and other male relatives joined us after traveling the entire distance from Pakistan to India on foot with a caravan. We were overwhelmed with gratitude.

We spent the next few months in homes abandoned by Muslim families who had fled to Pakistan to escape the raging communal fury in India. Our

ATHENAEUM *Indianapolis, Indiana*

RAJASTHAN STREET SCENE, INDIA

grandfather was devastated. We were frightened at the prospect of facing an uncertain future. I remember my father consoling Grandfather, "Bapujee (Father), by God's grace we have survived; we are alive; we will rebuild our lives again." I marvel at his courage, sense of optimism, and graceful acceptance of new challenges. With tireless determination, he rebuilt opportunities for his family on modest earnings.

As I look back, I see continued affirmations and unexpected gifts along the journey of my life. My father's inspiration and spirit shape my thoughts. I consider myself among the fortunate ones whom God and America have given another chance at life. I draw strength from reflections on my past. As I look forward, I hope to channel my gifts, lessons, and opportunities to make a difference.

The promise of life remains unfulfilled for many. Man has known and witnessed much pain and suffering in the past centuries. Recurring nightmares continue to traumatize nations and trample human dignity in many places. Such tragedies must end. We must all join in a caravan of hope, embrace the true spirit of our humanity, and share responsibility to expand peace and freedom for all. May our faith guide our steps.

ROCK TEMPLE *Tiruchi, India*

The Great Wall of China — Length 1500 Miles
Begun under Chow dynasty 4th and 3rd Century B.C. Completed under Ming dynasty 1368-1640 AD. *banwari Singh*
June 1984

GREAT WALL OF CHINA

35

By Your Grace

Lord, for reasons that You alone know
Your angels carried me across many an ordeal:
Fires of hell, darkness, genocide all around,
A drowning that was carrying me to certain death,
Countless failures, falls, that shocked my mortal spirit.

Each time Your angels lifted me into sunshine,
Taught new lessons, charged me to go forward:
Welcome another day; imagine a new beginning;
Your Compassion and Grace never left my side.

Lord, loss of beloved ones has shaken me;
 I face a deepening wound in spirit
Scars of the aftermath run deeper still.
The agony of uncertainty here and elsewhere,

Medieval Clock
Staré Město, Praha, Czechoslovakia   K.P.Singh

MEDIEVAL CLOCK *Prague, Czechoslovakia*

Disrupt the rhythms of my soul,
making unfamiliar music.
My songs and thoughts reveal a heart in pain
Stirring images of sadness.

Lord, I come to Your door in search of Light:
Faith, patience, courage, kindness of heart,
 True understanding, and seek blessed peace.
Dispel all doubt and temptations to unfair judgement;
Bless my struggle against unrewarding ends.

Let Your Presence and a boundless spirit
Guide my daily pursuits, each trial along my way.
Let me dwell in Light; know Your peace in all things.

Golden Temple, Amritsar, Punjab
India

Riverscape

GANGES RIVER *Benares, India*

As I sat along the banks of the Yamuna River roaring down the mountains at a Sikh pilgrimage site in North India, my mind traveled back in time. Like life, rivers are in perpetual motion as if to fulfill some unwritten destiny and have been the subject and scenes of many myths, legends, and landmark happenings throughout history. Major rivers, if only they could speak, have been a witness to the transformations of life and culture. Time has brought change and washed away much valuable evidence. The surviving architecture, fragments of heritage, and the present activity along river banks provide us some intriguing reflections and record of the past. Traditionally, the river cultures often carry a unique aura and rich attractions for the human mind and spirit.

Water is central to life. In some religious traditions, rivers are worshiped as living entities and gods. Rivers sustain and nurture valleys and plains, generating and breathing life in their path, sometimes causing havoc during floods, and always carving and providing spectacular settings for cities and civilizations. Rivers serve as ribbons of creative energy and cultural activity along their stretch. River corridors and settlements represent a distinct vision of interdependence and coexistence between nature and man.

Major rivers like the Yangtze, Ganges, Nile, Mississippi, Amazon, and others have served as bridges between cultures and civilizations. The famous river town of Varanasi, the "oldest continuously inhabited city in the world," is located on the Ganges River in India; the beautiful "eternal city" of Rome is located on the banks of the Tiber River in Italy. Both have flourished as major centers of faith, learning, arts, trade, and culture since ancient times. Over the centuries, many ideas, cultures, and influences converged over land and water to give these river towns their character and mystique.

San Giorgio Maggiore is located across the Grand Canal from San Marco in Venice (one of the world's most enchanting cities). This beautiful Church was designed by Andrea Palladio in 1556 in the form of two intersecting classic "temples" and reflects Baroque and neo-Classical architectural styles and influences.

San Giorgio Maggiore
Venice , Italy

Kanwar Prakash Singh
ⓒ 2003

BANKS OF THE
GANGES RIVER

Benares, India

ARCHITECTURAL TAPESTRIES

EVERY TOWN AND CITY IS a composite of diverse architectural styles, cultural and aesthetic influences, and unique features that give the community a special character and distinction. Outstanding buildings in the area reflect the significant history, heritage, cherished traditions, and vision of the community's inhabitants. In addition, invading armies, foreign occupants, and new immigrants have left their mark on the urban landscape of some towns and cities by introducing new styles and creativity inspired by their native culture and traditions.

The urban mosaic today is richly paneled with a colorful variety of architecture and inlayed with diverse expressions from many periods and cultures. In ancient cities, one can see the architectural spectrum stretch over many styles and centuries. One can also witness the design concepts, motifs, and functions change with time. In recent years, architectural heritage has suffered much neglect and loss. Many

LAFAYETTE, INDIANA

architectural treasures are totally overwhelmed by the surrounding developments.

Today, major efforts are underway in many cities to safeguard old monuments and ensure that the historic and contemporary buildings exist side by side as a proud legacy of the community. This heritage can be a source of pride, celebration, and a major attraction.

The drawings in this section celebrate our major community highlights: outstanding historic and contemporary landmarks, monuments and memorials that best reflect the history and pride, and other elements of community architectural and cultural fabric. The composite drawings often include buildings, segments, and design features that symbolically represent life, work, worship, celebration, education, heritage, and other unique and indigenous elements. The supporting text, often an integral part of the composition, captures an essence of community history, heritage, and spirit.

Spirit in Architecture

Sometimes a single element of art or architecture in a historic or natural site can symbolize a spirit of something unique and grand. A structure, statue, or visual feature can make a statement of wonder. Setting and landscape design can further enhance the singular character and beauty of such a monumental creation.

For many, the Taj Mahal of India represents an architectural jewel of unsurpassed beauty; St. Mark's in Venice, Italy evokes immense opulence; and the ancient temple ruins of Baalbeck, Lebanon are masterpieces of Roman excellence. For others, the temples at Khujaraho, India represent unique sensual pleasure and artistic achievement; the Kremlin in Moscow: power, mystery and intrigue; and the Chateaux in Loire Valley, France: lifestyles of the rich and famous. Undoubtedly, the Arch in St. Louis represents a marvel of engineering; the cliff dwellings at Mesa Verde: an environmentally sound and imaginative habitat; and the Golden Temple at Amritsar, India: a serene spiritual splendor.

GRAND PLACE *Brussels, Belgium*

Indianapolis: Planned in 1821 by
famed architect-planner Alexander
Ralston, the city inherited a very
classical plan and a rich tradition
of civic, secular, residential and
commercial-industrial architecture,
that today is challenging the vision
creativity and leadership of the
All American city.

Athenaeum
1972

Union Station

Christ Church Cathedral

Scottish Rite

Old IU Law School

State Capitol

City Market

Gate - Crownhill Cemetery

James Whitcomb
Riley Home

Morris Butler Home

Indiana Theatre

Indianapolis I

Ganwar P. Singh

INDIANAPOLIS I, INDIANA

43

In addition, there are countless magnificent urban spaces (Grand Place, Brussels, Belgium), fountains (Trevi Fountain, Rome), and statues (Michelangelo's Pieta, Rome, Statue of Liberty, New York, and Seated Buddha, Kamakura, Japan). Many unique bridges (Golden Gate Bridge, San Francisco), gateways (Buddhist Stupa Gateway at Sanchi, India), and towers (Water Tower, Chicago) contribute beauty and spirit to our living landscapes. Countless intriguing structures (Great Wall of China), hallowed walls (the Wailing Wall, Jerusalem), and grand entrances (Notre Dame Cathedral, Paris, and Chenakesava Temple at Belur, India) express intense emotion and creativity. Fascinating panels: intricate ceilings (Amber Palace at Jaipur, India), beautiful stained-glass windows (San Chappelle, Paris), marvelous mosaics (St. Louis Cathedral, St Louis), and awesome paintings (Sistine Chapel at the Vatican) capture our imagination. Each such encounter with the beauty and greatness around us may leave imprints of new inspirations on our mind and spirit.

STATE CAPITOL BUILDING *Indianapolis, Indiana*

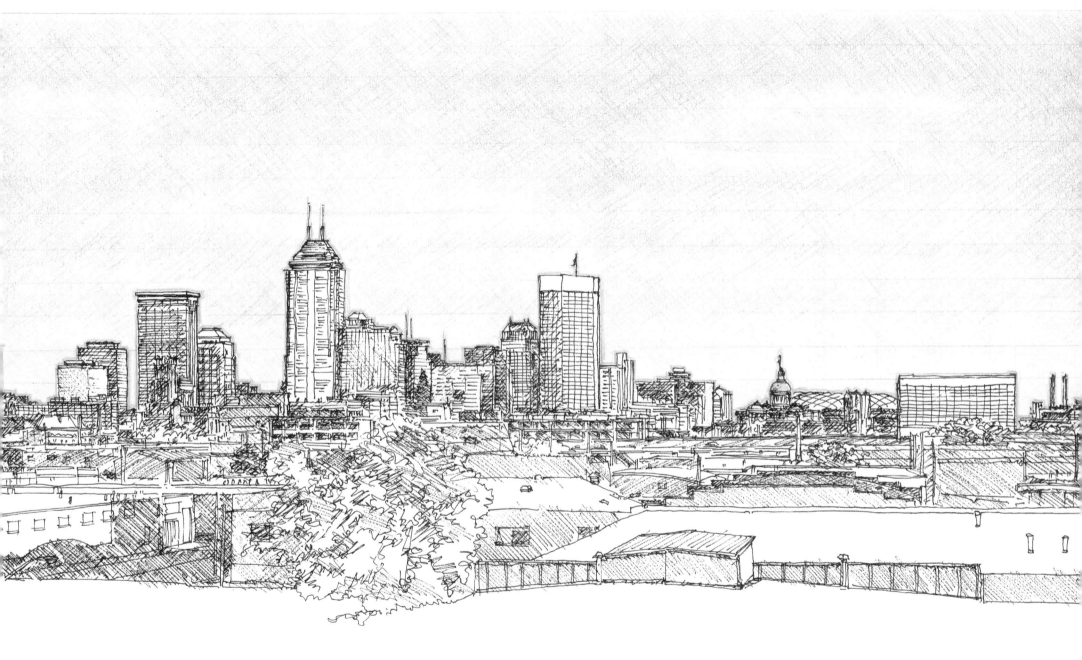

Indianapolis Skyline (View from the North)

Kanwar Prakash Singh
© 1995

The Spirit Is Nurtured in an Urban Setting

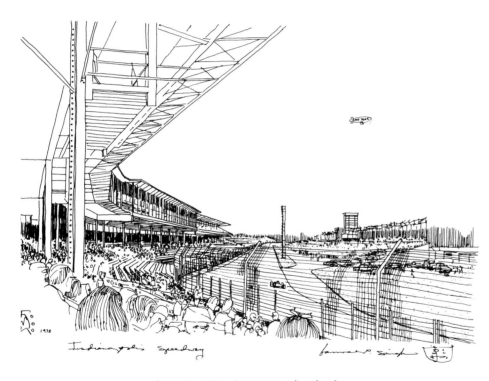

INDIANAPOLIS SPEEDWAY *Indianapolis, Indiana*

Cities around the world suffer from overcrowding, environmental pollution, and vanishing open spaces, creating an intense debate to improve the quality of our living environment. Imagination, innovation, and preservation provide answers. Unused railroad tracks, abandoned properties, undeveloped riverbanks, and wooded areas are being adapted as greenways and hiking trails. The Monon Trail in Indianapolis, the corridor that once carried trains, has undergone a remarkable transformation and has emerged as a growing community attraction.

Thousands of residents of all ages enjoy this beautifully landscaped trail to ride bikes, jog, meet friends, and be part of nature in the heart of an urban setting. The Monon provides an inviting space for recreation, stimulates the senses, and nurtures the spirit.

The ever-changing festival of nature on the trail--wildflowers, the frolic of God's creatures, the dance of light, the whisper of the wind and the spirit of the trail users--reassures us of blessings and treasures all around. The trail passes over brightly painted bridges that span the White River and the historic Broad Ripple Canal. Below is a haven for ducks, birds, and other animals amidst the flora, fauna, and sandy islands.

PIPER'S ALLEY, CHICAGO

1974

PIPER'S ALLEY *Chicago, Illinois*

It is delightful to see young mothers jogging behind baby carriages with little passengers simply enjoying the "moving" experience. Teenage friends and spirited seniors use the trail in remarkable tolerance and acceptance of everyone's space and pace. One feels a sense of kinship with strangers.

Morning sun filters through thick foliage and dances across the greenway. Tree branches stretch across and touch high above, creating an arched, lush canopy shading the corridor. One feels the aura of a cathedral with wildflowers and rich vegetation serving as sacred offerings and the songs of the birds and mysterious sounds of insects as the background music at the worship. Sikh scriptures affirm, "all Nature meditates."

A contemplative spirit descends and transports our thoughts to God's majesty and light in all things. Reciting the sacred Japji, the Sikh morning prayer, I imagine countless prayers flowing from natural canopies, cathedrals, and sacred sites everywhere toward heaven and converging at the Court of the Architect of all Creation.

CHAMBER OF COMMERCE BUILDING *Indianapolis, Indiana*

INDIANA

ORICAL DRUG STORE & PHAR

Hook's

FOOT LONG WITH CHILI SAUCE

FOOT LONG WITH CHILI SAUCE

POSTAL
TELEGRAPH
OFFICE
CABLEGRAMS

CORN DOGS

DRINK

MACHINERY
FIELD

STATE FAIR
TRASH

Indiana State Fair is a unique showcase of an important segment of
Indiana life, creativity and
economy. It is always colorful,
exciting, entertaining, educational
and fun.

The first state fair was held in 1852
in Military Park near downtown. The
fair moved to its present location
in 1892.

Indiana State Fair

Sanwar P. Singh

August 1976

INDIANA STATE FAIR

49

THE PRESENT COLUMBIA
CLUB BUILDING IS THE THIRD CLUB-
HOUSE TO OCCUPY THIS HISTORIC SITE.
FOUNDED IN 1889, THE COLUMBIA CLUB WAS
ORGANIZED BY A MARCHING SOCIETY CAMPAIGNING FOR THE
ELECTION OF BENJAMIN HARRISON TO THE WHITE HOUSE. THE STRUCTURE
THAT COLUMBIANS HAVE CALLED HOME SINCE 1925 WAS DESIGNED BY ARCHITECTS RUBISH
& HUNTER. THE STYLE IS REMINISCENT OF THE TRADITIONAL PERIOD OF LATE GOTHIC AND
EARLY RENAISSANCE ARCHITECTURE. THE BUILDING WAS PLACED ON THE NATIONAL
REGISTER OF HISTORIC PLACES IN 1983.
The Columbia Club at Monument Circle
Indianapolis, Indiana
James P. Singh
October 1985

THE COLUMBIA CLUB AT MONUMENT CIRCLE *Indianapolis, Indiana*

Each of us may see such "trails" in our own distinct spirit and light. Walking on the trail reminds me of the special times with my father while growing up in India. Walking was a way of life then. Our father taught us about life, nature, faith, and family. It is wonderful to see many families on the trail. In a fast-changing world, such simple traditional pursuits are a powerful anchor and a lasting rewarding gift to our spirit.

Greenways and natural sanctuaries must be an essential part of our community fabric in today's crowded cities. The Monon Trail offers a simple, creative, and imaginative example.

Imagine some day such "people corridors" linking generations, neighborhoods, and communities. They could serve as a bridge to a more tolerant, friendly, and healthy world. In nature may rest our best "causeway" to the sanctum of hope, promise, and peaceful coexistence for all living beings.

CHRIST CHURCH CATHEDRAL - 1860

MERCHANTS PLAZA

SOLDIERS AND SAILORS MONUMENT - 1902

CHILDREN'S MUSEUM - 1972

STATE CAPITOL BUILDING - 1888

RILEY HOME - 1872

HOOSIER DOME HOME OF INDIANAPOLIS COLTS - 1984

OLDFIELDS AT THE INDIANAPOLIS MUSEUM OF ART - 1912

CIRCLE THEATER - 1916
HOME OF INDIANAPOLIS SYMPHONY ORCHESTRA

INDIANAPOLIS IS ALIVE - PULSATING WITH EXCITEMENT , NEW AND RENEWED VITALITY - OFFERS OPPORTUNITIES , CHALLENGES AND SERVICES FOR A FULLER LIFE FOR ALL ITS CITIZENS. THE ALL-AMERICAN CITY CELEBRATES ITS PROUD PAST , ITS ETHNIC HERITAGE AND UNIQUE CULTURE , AS IT VIGOROUSLY AND CREATIVELY PURSUES SOLUTIONS TO FUTURE NEEDS AND CHALLENGES, SETTING THE PACE FOR CITIES ACROSS THE NATION UNDER ITS ABLE , DEDICATED AND IMAGINATIVE CITY, STATE AND COMMUNITY LEADERSHIP . INDIANAPOLIS IS ON THE MOVE . IT IS A CITY WITH A PROMISE . INDIANAPOLIS IS A NEW EXPERIENCE TODAY .

Indianapolis, Indiana , U.S.A.

© April 30, 1985

At Peace with Nature

Populations are on the move. People are converging in new promised lands. The rhythms of life itself are undergoing transition due to population explosions and technological pressures. Troubling major conflicts, cultural confrontations, and exploitation of natural resources are adversely affecting our environment and life throughout the global village. Man himself poses the greatest threat to the survival of all living beings. Creating a safe and healthy environment for all people may be one answer.

Nature in all its beauty, diversity, rhythms, and cycles is a formidable presence around us. Nature has always generously shared riches that provided sanctuary to man and challenged many to acts of daring and adventure. Painters, poets, photographers, and divinely inspired souls understand the power and mystery of nature. American scholars Ralph Waldo Emerson and Henry David Thoreau portray nature as an integral part of the universal whole with lessons and inspirations for the human mind and spirit. No wonder that we find nature in art, music, dance, literature, worship, lifestyles, architecture, design, and other creative forms.

DEPEW FOUNTAIN
University Park, Indianapolis   Kanwal Prakash Singh
© august 1988

DEPEW FOUNTAIN *Indianapolis, Indiana*

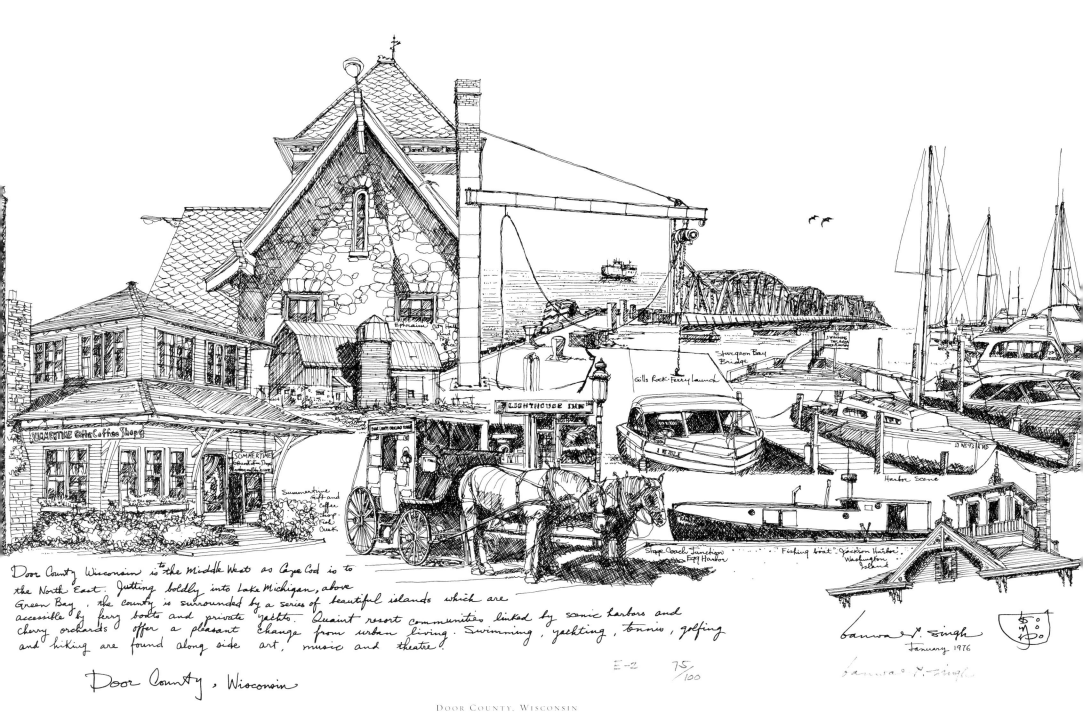

Ephraim

Sturgeon Bay Bridge

Gills Rock Ferry Launch

LIGHTHOUSE INN

SUMMERTIME Gifts Coffee Shops

SUMMERTIME Gift and Coffee Shop Harbor and the River

Summertime Gift and Coffee Shop Fish Creek

Harbor Scene

Stage Coach Junction Egg Harbor

Fishing boat · Jackson Harbor Washington Island

Door County Wisconsin is to the Middle West as Cape Cod is to the North East. Jutting boldly into Lake Michigan, above Green Bay, the county is surrounded by a series of beautiful islands which are accessible by ferry boats and private yachts. Quaint resort communities linked by scenic harbors and cherry orchards offer a pleasant change from urban living. Swimming, yachting, tennis, golfing and hiking are found along side art, music and theatre.

Door County, Wisconsin

Sanwa P. Singh
January 1976

E-2   75/100

Sanwa P. Singh

Nature, besides sustaining life, offers a mirror to our existence and defines our relationship with the universe. Man is beginning to recognize the importance of ecology and the rich offerings of nature for human well-being. Man must create harmony for life, embrace and cherish nature as a friend, and preserve the beauty and sanctity of nature as a true gift and image of the divine. In nature and through nature may lie the causeway to the sanctum of hope, promise, and peace for all living beings. Creating and sharing the universal promise of a safe environment for life with all cultures under the one blue sky is the key to our survival as a human species.

KNIGHTSTOWN, INDIANA

COUNTY COURTHOUSE - DANVILLE

OLD ST. MALACHY CHURCH - BROWNSBURG

HISTORICAL MUSEUM - DANVILLE

OLD SCHOOL HOUSE - BROWNSBURG

WESTERN YEARLY MEETINGHOUSE -PLAINFIELD

OLD HAUNTED BRIDGE - OFF US 36

LOCATED CENTRALLY, WEST OF THE STATE CAPITAL AT INDIANAPOLIS (POP. 800,000) HENDRICKS COUNTY WAS NAMED AFTER GOVERNOR WILLIAM HENDRICKS WHO WAS THE SECOND GOVERNOR (1822-1825) OF INDIANA. HENDRICKS COUNTY WAS OFFICIALLY ORGANIZED BY AN ACT OF THE INDIANA STATE GENERAL ASSEMBLY WHICH BECAME EFFECTIVE IN 1824.
THE COUNTY HAS A TOTAL AREA OF 417 SQUARE MILES AND AN ESTIMATED POPULATION OF 64,600 IN 1977. THE TEN INCORPORATED TOWNS IN THE COUNTY ARE AMO, BROWNSBURG, CLAYTON, COATESVILLE, DANVILLE, LIZTON, NORTH SALEM, PITTSBORO, PLAINFIELD AND STILESVILLE. PREDOMINATELY A RURAL COUNTY, IT HAS MANY UNIQUE AND HISTORIC ARCHITECTURAL LANDMARKS. THE HENDRICKS COUNTY BANK AND TRUST COMPANY IS PROUD TO HAVE HAD THE PRIVILEGE OF SERVING THE RESIDENTS OF THE COUNTY SINCE 1908.

Hendricks County, Indiana

Laneware Singh
March 1, 1980

HENDRICKS COUNTY, INDIANA

A Window to Life and Legacy

Architecture is more than an envelope of space or a shelter for human activity and interaction. Architecture provides us a window, visual introduction, and insight into human thought. Through architecture, which represents a festive spectrum of our life and legacy, we witness many diverse and distinct highlights of building adventures at different periods in history.

Architecture offers physical evidence of people and their cultures. It is a three-dimensional study of diverse patterns for living, worship, work, and celebrations. Architecture reveals imaginative responses and adaptations to provide a safe and stimulating environment for human needs, experiences, and advancement.

There is a special spirit present in architecture. It is evident in Nature's grand cathedrals of canyons, valleys

Holy Rosary Church   Market Square Are /City County Bldg.   Union Station   Hoosier Dome / Pan. Am. Plaza   Penrod Artfair at Oldfields

INDIANAPOLIS

and mountain tops, in the man-made mansions of grandeur, in the very modest places to live, work, worship, and gather, and everything in between. Our architectural heritage remains central to our community and national image.

Our spirit gravitates toward the magnificent sacred places of worship, palatial buildings, majestic enclosures, and serene gardens that proclaim splendor. Landscaped corridors delightfully interrupted by imposing statues of the famous, festive fountains and spectacular piazzas lined with great shopping arcades, and sidewalk cafés offer a sense of the times and inspirations that shaped them.

Often embellished with ornamental designs and motifs, colorful decorations and visual surprises, historical architecture captures our imagination and demands special attention. Our sacred landmarks are also often treasure houses of artistic excellence and cultural insights.

Architecture is a living theatre, a physical, visual, and spatial creation designed to enhance life experiences.

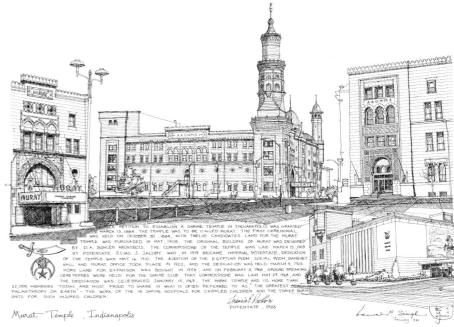

MURAT TEMPLE *Indianapolis, Indiana*

CITY MARKET
VICTORIAN IN STYLE

CITY MARKET

TOMLINSON HALL ARCH
RESTORED CITY MARKET REDEDICATED IN SEPTEMBER 1977. (INTERIOR)

BUILT IN 1886 AND DESIGNED BY ARCHITECT D.A. BOHLEN , THE PRESENT MARKET HOUSE STANDS ON THE SITE RESERVED FOR A MARKET IN THE ALEXANDER RALSTON'S PLAN OF 1821 FOR THE "TOWN OF INDIANAPOLIS". THE SIMPLE BRICK EXTERIOR PROVIDES AN INTERESTING CONTRAST TO THE INTERIOR OF THE CITY MARKET WITH ITS BEAUTIFULLY DESIGNED FRESH FOOD STALLS , WROUGHT IRON AND IRON TRUSSES SUPPORTING A RAISED CENTRAL GABLE CLERESTORY ROOF.
OVER THE YEARS , THE MARKET HAS GONE THROUGH MANY CHANGES AND CHALLENGES WHICH IN RECENT YEARS THREATENED ITS VERY SURVIVAL AS A DOWNTOWN LANDMARK OF DISTINCTION . THE HISTORIC CITY MARKET TODAY IS A CENTER-PIECE OF MARKET SQUARE COMPLEX THANKS TO THE IMAGINATION AND COMMITMENT OF MR. FRANK J. MURRAY (MARKET MASTER 1968-76) , HON'BLE RICHARD G. LUGAR (MAYOR 1968-76) , STANDHOLDERS AND MARKET PATRONS AND LILLY ENDOWMENT WHICH PROVIDED $4,751,000 TOWARDS THE MARKET RESTORATION.

Indianapolis City Market

banwar P. Singh
august 1982

INDIANAPOLIS CITY MARKET, INDIANA

59

Architecture places wonder and achievement within our sight for daily discovery. Architecture links our spirit to the past, anchors our thoughts to the present, and transports our mind to the future.

Architecture provides a vast encyclopedia of culture as it relates to the art and science of building in human civilization. Formidable forts, "Great Walls," and citadels were built to keep ill winds and dangers away, protecting the safety and liberty of individuals and institutions, and the sanctity of historic treasures and heritage sites. Many architectural gems have been lost forever to the ravages of time, neglect, and unfortunate shortsightedness. Today, the architectural mosaic of humanity has many missing panels. Throughout history, the burning, looting, and plundering the important heritage of the vanquished was a cruel way to rob people of their dignity and culture and demoralize the conquered people. One can witness the scars of this calculated tyranny in all cultures and corners of the world.

The past can never be an excuse for future apathy. Each of us has a special responsibility to support our architectural heritage as a collective trust and commitment

FORT WAYNE, INDIANA

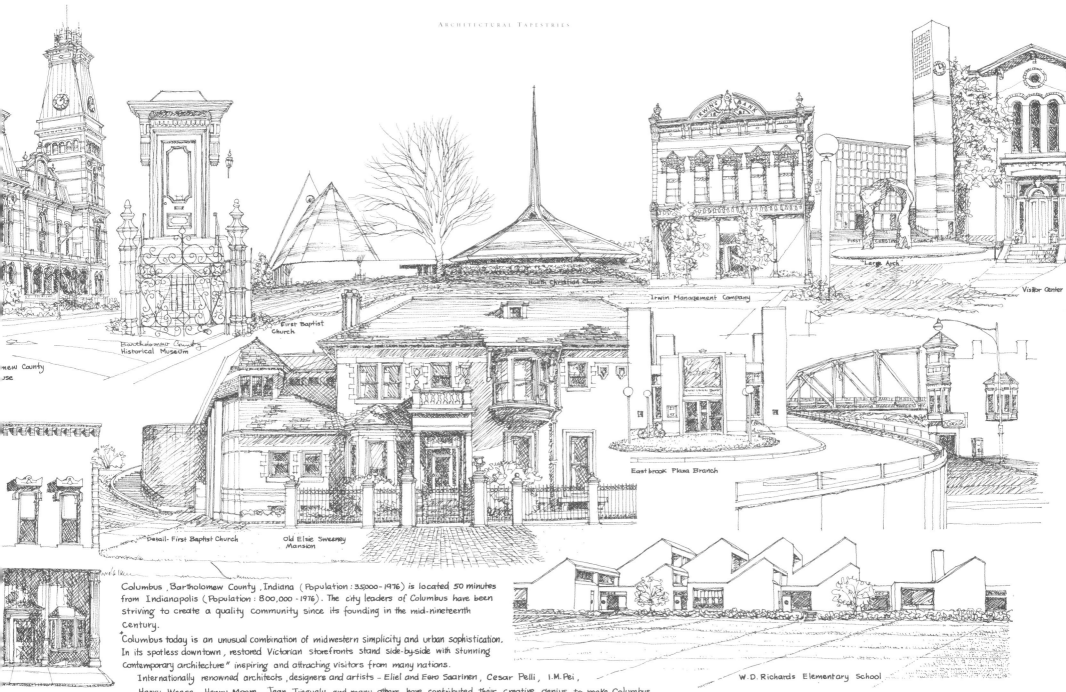

North Christian Church

Irwin Management Company

"Large Arch"

FIRST CHRISTIAN CHURCH

Visitor Center

First Baptist Church

Bartholomew County Historical Museum

Bartholomew County House

Eastbrook Plaza Branch

Detail - First Baptist Church

Old Elsie Sweeney Mansion

W.D. Richards Elementary School

Columbus, Bartholomew County, Indiana (Population: 35,000 - 1976) is located 50 minutes from Indianapolis (Population: 800,000 - 1976). The city leaders of Columbus have been striving to create a quality community since its founding in the mid-nineteenth century.

"Columbus today is an unusual combination of midwestern simplicity and urban sophistication. In its spotless downtown, restored Victorian storefronts stand side-by-side with stunning contemporary architecture" inspiring and attracting visitors from many nations.

Internationally renowned architects, designers and artists - Eliel and Eero Saarinen, Cesar Pelli, I.M. Pei, Harry Weese, Henry Moore, Jean Tinguely and many others have contributed their creative genius to make Columbus America's architectural showcase. and earned for it many honors and architectural awards including the Total Design Award from the National Society of Interior Design for exemplifying "environmental rebirth". and an A.I.A citation - Columbus as "the best possible example of how architecture can improve the physical environment and quality of life of a community."

Columbus, Indiana

Sanwar A. Singh
October 1977

to future generations. It is heartening to see international organizations today engaged in saving entire cities such as Venice and restoring designated sites throughout the world under the leadership of UNESCO. Humanity is engaged in building friendly "bridges" that span huge physical, cultural, and spiritual divides and pave new passageways to interconnect our shared heritage and destiny. Nations, cities, and people are engaged in integrating their past into future fabrics of communities

Today, the opportunity exists to learn new techniques and develop creative ideas from one another to build imaginative enclosures and beautiful "canopies" for human needs and endeavors. Thanks to science and technology, the preservation, restoration, and rediscovery of endangered architectural heritage has taken on new urgency. Man cannot afford to lose this window to the past and unique spectrum of life and human legacy.

OBLESIK SQUARE OF WAR MEMORIAL PLAZA

SCOTTISH-RITE CATHEDRAL *Indianapolis, Indiana*

GREENFIELD, THE
COUNTY SEAT OF
HANCOCK COUNTY,
IS LOCATED
TWENTY MILES EAST OF THE STATE CAPITAL OF INDIANAPOLIS.

FOUNDED IN 1828 AND NAMED FOR THE ABUNDANT FERTILE LAND, GREENFIELD IS HOME TO APPROXIMATELY 14000 RESIDENTS. THE VIBRANT DOWNTOWN IS SITUATED ON US 40,
THE NATIONAL ROAD.
A PROSPEROUS FARMING ECONOMY, INDUSTRY, AND OTHER FORMS OF BUSINESS INCLUDING WORLD RENOWNED MEDICAL RESEARCH FLOURISH IN GREENFIED. GREENFIED HAS MANY HISTORIC AND ARCHITECTURAL
LANDMARKS INCLUDING THE BIRTHPLACE OF JAMES WHITCOMB RILEY. RILEY, THE FAMOUS HOOSIER POET, SO APTLY PROCLAIMED, "GREENFIELD IS MY HOME AND YOUR HOME AND YOUR PARENTS' HOME
AND THE BEST HOME OUTSIDE of HEAVEN."
LOCATED IN THE HEART OF HISTORIC DOWNTOWN GREENFIELD, THE GREATER GREENFIELD CHAMBER OF COMMERCE IS PROUD TO HAVE SERVED THE COMMUNITY SINCE 1957.

Greenfield, Indiana USA

Kanwar Prakash Singh
© 1998

Vision 2001

MUNCIE - DELAWARE COUNTY
CHAMBER of COMMERCE

CITY OF MUNCIE INDIANA
1865

MUNCIE AND THE SURROUNDING TOWNS OF
INDIANA WERE HOME TO THE GREAT
LATE 19TH. AND EARLY 20TH. CENTURIES
OF NATURAL GAS AND MUNCIE'S PROXIMITY.
BROUGHT MANY BUSINESSES AND
REFLECTS THAT LOCAL HISTORY.
MANUFACTURING, AND BALL STATE UNIVERSITY HAVE LEFT THEIR

EAST CENTRAL
GAS BOOM OF
THE DISCOVERY
TO WHITE RIVER
INDUSTRIES TO THE AREA, MUCH OF THE EXISTING ARCHITECTURE
AGRICULTURE, GLASS PRODUCTION, AUTOMOTIVE PARTS
MARK ON THE LANDSCAPE OF MUNCIE AND DELAWARE COUNTY.

MINNETRISTA PARKWAY

Muncie - Delaware County, USA

Kanwar Prakash Singh
© 2000

MUNCIE, INDIANA

64

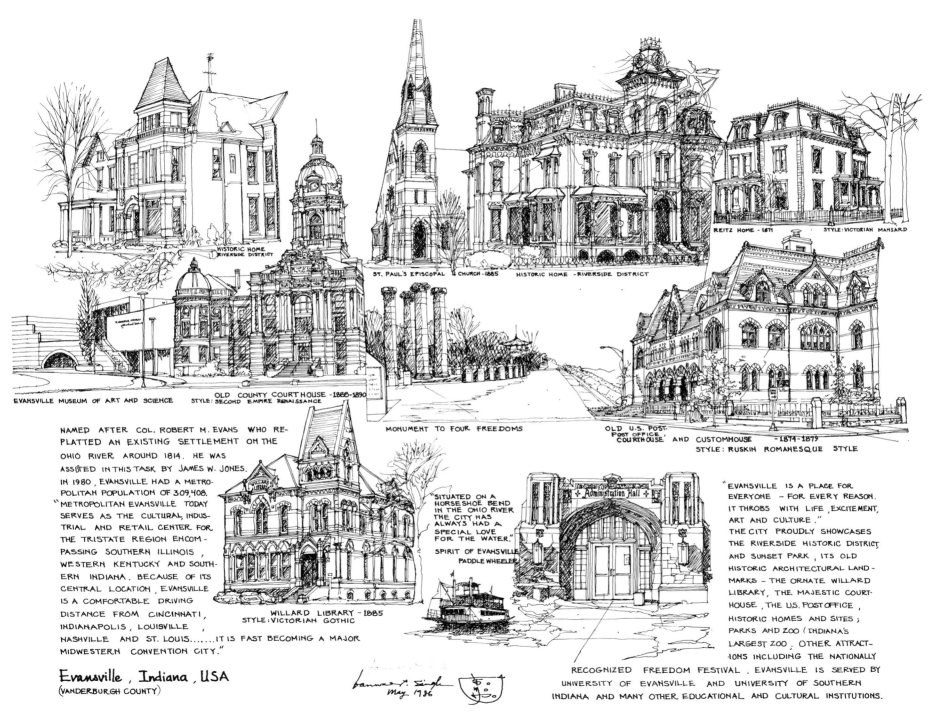

HISTORIC HOME
RIVERSIDE DISTRICT

REITZ HOME - 1871   STYLE: VICTORIAN MANSARD

ST. PAUL'S EPISCOPAL CHURCH-1885   HISTORIC HOME - RIVERSIDE DISTRICT

EVANSVILLE MUSEUM OF ART AND SCIENCE   OLD COUNTY COURTHOUSE -1888-1890
STYLE: SECOND EMPIRE RENAISSANCE

MONUMENT TO FOUR FREEDOMS

OLD U.S. POST-
POST OFFICE
COURTHOUSE AND CUSTOMHOUSE   -1874-1879
STYLE: RUSKIN ROMANESQUE STYLE

NAMED AFTER COL. ROBERT M. EVANS WHO RE-
PLATTED AN EXISTING SETTLEMENT ON THE
OHIO RIVER AROUND 1814. HE WAS
ASSISTED IN THIS TASK BY JAMES W. JONES.
IN 1980, EVANSVILLE HAD A METRO-
POLITAN POPULATION OF 309,408.
"METROPOLITAN EVANSVILLE TODAY
SERVES AS THE CULTURAL, INDUS-
TRIAL AND RETAIL CENTER FOR
THE TRISTATE REGION ENCOM-
PASSING SOUTHERN ILLINOIS,
WESTERN KENTUCKY AND SOUTH-
ERN INDIANA. BECAUSE OF ITS
CENTRAL LOCATION, EVANSVILLE
IS A COMFORTABLE DRIVING
DISTANCE FROM CINCINNATI,
INDIANAPOLIS, LOUISVILLE,
NASHVILLE AND ST. LOUIS.......IT IS FAST BECOMING A MAJOR
MIDWESTERN CONVENTION CITY."

Evansville, Indiana, USA
(VANDERBURGH COUNTY)

WILLARD LIBRARY - 1885
STYLE: VICTORIAN GOTHIC

"SITUATED ON A
HORSESHOE BEND
IN THE OHIO RIVER
THE CITY HAS
ALWAYS HAD A
SPECIAL LOVE
FOR THE WATER."

SPIRIT OF EVANSVILLE
PADDLE WHEELER

Administration Hall

"EVANSVILLE IS A PLACE FOR
EVERYONE - FOR EVERY REASON.
IT THROBS WITH LIFE, EXCITEMENT,
ART AND CULTURE."
THE CITY PROUDLY SHOWCASES
THE RIVERSIDE HISTORIC DISTRICT
AND SUNSET PARK, ITS OLD
HISTORIC ARCHITECTURAL LAND-
MARKS - THE ORNATE WILLARD
LIBRARY, THE MAJESTIC COURT-
HOUSE, THE U.S. POST OFFICE,
HISTORIC HOMES AND SITES;
PARKS AND ZOO (INDIANA'S
LARGEST ZOO; OTHER ATTRACT-
IONS INCLUDING THE NATIONALLY
RECOGNIZED FREEDOM FESTIVAL. EVANSVILLE IS SERVED BY
UNIVERSITY OF EVANSVILLE AND UNIVERSITY OF SOUTHERN
INDIANA AND MANY OTHER EDUCATIONAL AND CULTURAL INSTITUTIONS.

banwari l. Singh
May 1986

EVANSVILLE, INDIANA

GOLDEN TEMPLE

Amritsar, India

CATHEDRALS *of* SPIRIT

RELIGIOUS ARCHITECTURE reflects and affirms the great importance of faith in the lives of people. Throughout the centuries, man has spared no effort to create impressive structures, to pursue the highest artistic achievements, and to design awe-inspiring worship spaces. Sometimes, man has captured a mystic and indescribable aura that seems to touch the threshold between temporal and divine.

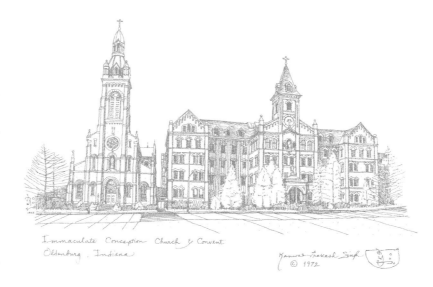

IMMACULATE CONCEPTION CHURCH *Oldenburg, Indiana*

monuments created by man. In addition, sacred architecture enshrines a rich and colorful spectrum of the greatest fine and decorative arts of humanity.

Our sacred shrines are often centers of learning, history, heritage, and pilgrimage. They are repositories of artistic treasures, sacred relics, and records of the faith community. Many famous shrines are located on beautiful sites, in magnificent cathedrals of

Our sacred architecture provides an environment to introduce and uplift the human spirit to higher realms and celebrate the glory and grandeur of the Creator and creation as proclaimed in distinct faith traditions.

Sacred architecture often mirrors our cultural and ethnic heritage. Religious architecture adopted and often invented architectural styles, building innovations, and artistic creations to celebrate and nurture our deepest spiritual needs. Our sacred heritage represents some of the grandest architectural

nature, and offer attractions to inspire the body, mind, and spirit.

The drawings on the following pages introduce sacred places of Christian, Jewish, Sikh, Buddhist, Hindu, Jain, Moslem, Bahai, and other faith traditions. These sacred places are located on many continents and represent very diverse architectural styles across several centuries and cultures. The accompanying text shares reflections on matters of faith, spirituality, life, inspiration, arts, and the culture of worship.

Tapestry of Faith

The drawing titled "Cathedrals of Spirit" celebrates through art a universal thought revealed and affirmed by the Sikh scriptures and many other religions. The Sikh faith proclaims that "God is the Fountainhead of all divine knowledge, all languages, and is the inspiration of all faith traditions" embraced and cherished by man.

Understanding, appreciating, and celebrating the diverse cultural, ethnic, and spiritual traditions of people everywhere are important to the peaceful co-existence of humanity. Learning about other faith traditions can greatly enhance our understanding of matters of spirit.

On close examination, we discover an amazing unity in spirit and interests among people and faiths. Unmistakable threads bind us one to the other, affirming our shared destiny as living beings. Our spiritual differences and cultural distinctions

BUDDIST TEMPLE *Bangkok, Thailand*

suddenly appear less important in the light of their divine origin and are common concerns.

Our cherished dreams of a world at peace must recognize and respect the inspirations that are a part of the global spiritual landscape today. As a leader of the free world, America must assure equal justice, dignity, opportunity to all diverse ideas and sacred ideals, and to all people who aspire, strive, and struggle to succeed in capturing their own American dream. "Cathedrals of Spirit," a composite drawing, introduces us to diverse sacred architecture from many continents, generations, and faiths and reminds us of our shared humanity and collective sacred heritage. The drawing further reinforces man's inspired and grand visions to build magnificent sacred structures for religious worship.

The Church of St Mary Magdalene

The Dome of The Rock, Jerusalem
"Laa Ilaaha illa Ilaah! There is no god but God!"
—Holy Koran
"Allah is the Creator of all things, and of all things He is the Guardian."

St. Peter's Basilica, Rome

Golden Temple, Amritsar
"His stars are strung across the mighty skies His Light and Radiance illuminate the unfathomable Heavens."
—The Sikh Scriptures

Shalom
"Truth is only One. They call Him by different Names." –The Vedas

Eastern Torana Gateway Sanchi

Church of The Holy Sepulchre Jerusalem

Bahai Temple, Chicago

Ancient Hindu Temple, Trichinapalli
"However Far My Eye May Wander Thou Standest Before me! For the Heavens and the Splendor of the stars Are Thy Image!"
- Hala Satavahana

"The Heavens declare the Glory of God; and the firmament Sheweth His handiwork."
– Holy Bible – Psalm 19

"God Created Light in the Beginning From the Light He Created All Life."

The Western Wall, Jerusalem
"Let them make Me a Sanctuary that I may dwell among them."
– Exodus, Ch.25, V.8

God's Divine Messengers brought the message of Love, Peace and the unity of the human spirit to our earth.

Buddhist Temple Bangkok

Christ Church Cathedral Indianapolis

"...With a boundless mind should one cherish all living beings; radiating friendliness over the entire world, above, below and all around without limit;" – the Metta Sutra

The architects of faith built majestic Cathedrals, Temples, Mosques, Synagogues, Shrines to honor The Supreme Creator and to worship and celebrate their faith. They sanctified natural sites and objects and sought Divine benevolence and paid homage to their gods.

Today, as our best preserved architecture, these "Cathedrals of Spirit" provide us a glimpse of the spiritual heritage, Creative genius and legacy of man. They enshrine the greatest cultural, religious and artistic traditions and inspirations of the times in which they were built and rebuilt or restored to original grandeur. They help us understand the journey of human civilization through the ages. They enrich our cities with their beauty and their majesty. These magnificient landmarks and sites are the heart and soul of human experience.

We must assure the right of each individual to make his/her "pilgrimage" to these "places of bliss" in peace. The preservation of these treasures is the collective responsibility of all mankind.

Jain Temple, Ahmadabad

"Cathedrals of Spirit"

Kanwal Prakash Singh
© October 1994

The composite drawing highlights holy places and sites from distant lands and distinct and unfamiliar architectural styles. The drawing also incorporates sacred text that reverberates with divine images and inspirations of major world religions. By hand-coloring the prints, I introduce the viewer to the rich embellishments that are an integral part of these sacred sites, connecting the human imagination to the awesome splendor of the heavens.

The "Cathedrals of Spirit" composite drawing is an artistic creation to represent and celebrate the rich tapestry of faiths. The drawing is both an introduction and an invitation to appreciate and celebrate the collective spiritual heritage of mankind.

PAMPAPATI TEMPLE *Hampi, India*

Christ Church Cathedral
Indianapolis

Kanwal Prakash Singh
© 1984

CHRIST CHURCH CATHEDRAL *Indianapolis, Indiana*

Unity of Spirit

All living beings, threaded in one universal spirit
Cherish hope, friendship, and understanding.
Let us affirm tolerance of our unique individuality,
 Honor all peaceful expressions of our humanity.

Let us not be troubled by the growing diversity around us:
New ideas, inspirations, interests, and perspectives;
But by persisting expectations of conformity at this critical moment:
In a world of transcending thresholds and transforming promise.

God has created us in His image, yet made each person unique;
God's Love, Light, and Spirit manifested in all His Creation.
Recognize all Creation, all humanity as His reflection;
Part of the mystery, wonder, and splendor of His Majesty.

Let us see everyone worthy of dignity, respect;
Stretch our hand and spirit to understand one another,
Embrace and usher a New Renaissance of ideas, innovations;
Discover new creative energy to advance our visions of greatness.

Converging diversity of people, hopes, talents, traditions,
Enrich and expand tapestry of life, spirit, and culture;
Celebrate this colorful gathering as something inherently beautiful,
Harness its power to shape "a more perfect" vision for all humanity.

ST. PETER'S *Rome, Italy*

"ਡਿਠੇ ਸਭੇ ਥਾਵ ਨਹੀ ਤੁਧੁ ਜੇਹਾ" – ਗੁਰੂ ਗ੍ਰੰਥ ਸਾਹਿਬ
"Among places of bliss there is none like this" – Adi Granth

Golden Temple, Amritsar, India
(Indo-Sarasenic – 17th Century)

Kanwar Prakash Singh
April 13, 1985
ਕੰਵਰ ਪ੍ਰਕਾਸ਼ ਸਿੰਘ

Temples of Spirit

In sacred architecture, to enhance visual drama and aesthetics, we see imaginative adaptation of man-made, natural, and spiritual elements. Religious myths, history, and legends heighten the mystery and spiritual aura of our religious gathering places. In many traditions, sacred architecture is richly embellished with sculpture, stained-glass windows, lighting, paintings, murals, mosaics, tapestries, and other decorative treatments. These artistic creations offer symbolic interpretations, spiritual highlights, and celebrations of the awesome grandeur and mystery of the Divine. Sacred architecture attempts to stretch our imagination to the origin of major beliefs and traditions.

A religious center takes on added significance when the place is associated with a major faith-architect or founder, a landmark spiritual encounter, or some other defining moment in the history and journey of the faith. Historic structures set in beautiful surroundings declare and celebrate the importance of such sites and pilgrimage centers.

Many sacred shrines, cathedrals, synagogues, mosques, temples, and holy sites are located along ancient rivers, beautiful lakes, and oceanfronts, in gorgeous valleys, and high in the mountains. The environs lift our spirit high above the noise and temporal demands and distractions. Our mind and spirit surrender to the mysterious aura, the amazing elegance, and

BAHAI TEMPLE *Wilmette, Illinois*

the majesty of the place and the surroundings. The experience is divinely inspiring.

Our inspired state of mind finds deeper meaning and connections in our spiritual experience. Art serves as a medium of communication and inspiration. In European cathedrals, the richly decorated stained-glass windows choreograph the dance of light, color, and imagery in the sacred space. The masterful paintings and tapestries portray the real and imagined facets of faith history and spirituality. Majestic columns and facades with the statues of religious figures introduce events, associations, and relationships within the faith hierarchy.

In Sikh temples, the rich brocaded canopies, sacred scriptures and relics, priceless furnishings, wall and ceiling decorations, spatial design, and other elements all work in harmony of style and rhythm to submerge the faithful in reverence and devotion.

Outside the gilded domes and walls of the central edifice, reflecting sacred pools, inlaid marble floors, and transitional fixtures grace the complex. Majestic entrances and historic sites all around the landscaped ceremonial walkway contribute to the sensuous and marvelous magic of the place.

Sacred architecture offers us visual echoes of the cosmic splendor. Simultaneously, architecture expresses the adventure and journey of the building

ST. MARY'S CATHOLIC CHURCH - 1868

FORT WAYNE IS A CITY OF MANY
BEAUTIFUL PLACES OF WORSHIP.

ST. PAUL'S EVANGELICAL
LUTHERAN CHURCH - 1889

BLESSED VIRGIN MARY   —

CATHEDRAL OF THE IMMACULATE CONCEPTION - 1860
BLESSED SACRAMENT CHAPEL - 1950

Fort Wayne, Indiana, U.S.A

"Churches"

⁷⁄₂₅

Kanwal Prakash Singh
©   July 1990

Kanwal Prakash Singh

CHURCHES OF FORT WAYNE, INDIANA

arts and the art of building. It may reveal the essence of the times. Architecture may offer a startling glimpse of the beauty beyond our temporal experience. Architecture enshrines imagination and spirit that takes us to the outermost limits of the possible and the probable. Our intense preoccupation with the matters of spirit has challenged the arts, science, and technology to their very limits. The results speak for themselves.

Religious shrines represent a unique celebration of spirit, arts, and humanity. Many centers of pilgrimage advocate and affirm the faith-inspired tradition of harmony with the environment and the universe around us. "Nature resides in the Creator" and "Nature is the Crown of God."- The Sikh Scriptures

Religious centers throughout history have been major temples of learning and cathedrals of spirit. They have served as sanctuaries of refuge and fortresses of faith and renewal during uncertain times. Many of them have been the scenes of battles, great suffering, and desecration. The faithful have made incredible sacrifices to defend, preserve, and restore their sanctity. They are monuments of remembrance.

A religious center is a place to contemplate, connect in spirit, and commune with Nature in the Highest Supreme Immaculate Reality. In addition, it serves as a sanctuary for knowledge, learning of liturgical arts, study of scriptures, religious literature, and celebrated academies of fine arts and music. Many have served as monasteries for survival and the teaching of martial arts. Many serve as centers for social and community services and schools for learning and teaching about life, living, culture, and human civilization. Some have achieved distinction as a laboratory for innovation and

The Church of Convent Immaculate Conception - 1924
Ferdinand, Indiana
Style : Romanesque

Kanwal Prakash Singh
© August 1988

THE CHURCH OF CONVENT IMMACULATE CONCEPTION *Ferninand, Indiana*

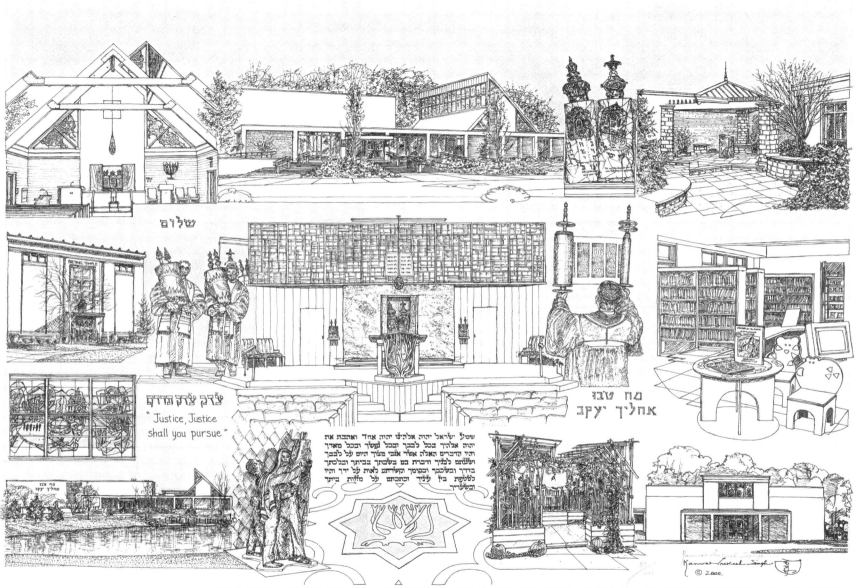

שלום

צֶדֶק צֶדֶק תִּרְדֹּף
"Justice, Justice
shall you pursue"

מה טבו
אהליך יעקב

CONGREGATION
BETH-EL ZEDECK

Indianapolis, Indiana, USA

BETH-EL ZEDECK AROSE IN 1928 FROM CONGREGATIONS BETH-EL AND OHEV ZEDECK. IN 1958 THE SYNAGOGUE MOVED FROM 34TH AND RUCKLE STREETS TO 600 WEST 70TH STREET. THE 1999 ROOTS & WINGS RENOVATION AND EXPANSION BROUGHT OUR CONGREGATION INTO THE 21ST CENTURY.

AT BETH-EL ZEDECK TRADITION AND RENEWAL GO HAND IN HAND.

AS בֵּית תְּפִלָּה - BEIT TEFILAH (HOUSE OF PRAYER), WE REACH FOR GOD; AS בֵּית מִדְרָשׁ - BEIT MIDRASH (HOUSE OF STUDY), WE REACH INTO OUR MINDS AND SOULS; AS בֵּית כְּנֶסֶת - BEIT KENESET (HOUSE OF FELLOWSHIP), WE REACH OUT TO OUR NEIGHBORS AND COMMUNITY.

CONGREGATION BETH-EL ZEDECK Indianapolis, Indiana

progress. Our sacred architecture has been a rich repository, a surviving link to our journey through the ages. It has been a crucible for social change and understanding of our humanity.

It would be too simplistic to suggest that our religion has been always a positive force for universal good. Religion has triggered many violent confrontations over crossing physical or spiritual boundaries. These factors are evident in the architectural choices and designs. Sacred heritage repeatedly fell victim to hate and suspicion of other faith traditions. Some rulers and bigoted zealots were convinced that they possessed the only right religious path.

Today, we are beginning to see all divine knowledge as our collective spiritual heritage. This realization offers us the best hope to preserve our diverse sacred architectural heritage for future generations, avoiding senseless destruction through ignorance, neglect, or design. Tough preservation policies and safeguards can make a lasting difference to save our heritage.

Our sacred architecture provides us a window to our spirit and civilization. World heritage sites must stay open to all. They are a testimony of the spiritual journeys in different faith traditions, the markers and milestones of human achievements. We cannot ignore their importance to each faith and to all humanity. We must preserve this resource as our collective architectural, artistic, and spiritual heritage.

North United Methodist Church
1925-1928 Architect: Charles H. Hopson, Atlanta, Georgia
The Tower of the Church was completed in 1973

NORTH UNITED METHODIST CHURCH *Indianapolis, Indiana*

The Cathedral Church of Saint Peter and Saint Paul towers above
the city of Washington from its stately site on Mount St. Alban. The magnificent
Gothic Cathedral, completed in 1990, is today a "House of Prayer for all People."

Washington National Cathedral
Washington D.C.

Kanwar Prakash Singh
© 2003

"Largest mosaic
collection in the world."

Named in honor of Saint Louis IX, King of France, the Cathedral's "unique design combines
architecture of Romanesque style on the exterior with wondrous Byzantine style interior."

Cathedral of Saint Louis – 1914

St. Louis, Missouri

Kanwal Prakash Singh
© 2000

CATHEDRAL OF SAINT LOUIS *St. Louis, Missouri*

Buddhist Temple
Benares, India

Lanwar P. Singh
January 1987

BUDDHIST TEMPLE *Benares, India*

Prayer as a Basic Act of Faith

All religions celebrate faith in special ways. Prayer is an integral part of our ceremonies and traditions. Prayer may be an act of salutation and praise of the Creator, a supplication for our human concerns and well being, or a petition for the good of humanity. It is a universal activity. Sikh Scriptures offer, "The entire creation resounds with prayer and celestial song."

Music, singing, recitation, chanting, meditation, reflection, dance, discourse, solitude, and silence are parts of worship and prayer services in many faiths. Flowers, incense, magnificent canopies, holy scriptures, religious art and embellishments, sacred symbols and rituals, ancient relics, and the architecture of sacred space create the spirit and the finer traditions of each faith.

Each element of prayer has a special meaning and significance to reach deep into the religious response of the devotee. The temporal elements of worship have a symbolic connection with and inspiration in our celestial origin as revealed by the sacred writings of all faiths.

> *"In the beginning, Allah created the Light*
> *By His might He created all.*
> *The entire universe is created from that one Light."*
> *- Sikh Scriptures: Muslim Saint Kabir*

SECOND PRESBYTERIAN CHURCH *Indianapolis, Indiana*

God is often referred to as Immaculate Reality, Waheguru, Wonderful Lord, Eternal Truth, Allah, Ishwar, Yehweh, Wakan Tanka, Universal Soul, and thousands of other glorious names and attributes. He sent Divine Messengers to enlighten us, teach us about the Creator and how to offer praise to Him. Thus, began the human spiritual journey.

Prayer took on many and varied dimensions and colorful expressions as the "architects of faith" built magnificent cathedrals, mosques, synagogues, gurudwaras, monasteries, pagodas, and other sanctuaries and sacred sites to pray to and honor the Creator. The worship practice in some traditions includes heavenly bodies, natural elements and forces, gods and goddesses, animals and mythological beings, man-made creations, historical sites, and divinely inspired scriptures, and spiritual treasures.

All religions command us to pray to and praise the Creator or a higher Power. Christ taught His disciples the "Lord's Prayer," which captures the essence of what we should be asking from God, the Father. Muslims recite Namaaz (sacred prayer) five times a day and offer praise and thanksgiving to Allah. Sikhs are instructed to remember God twenty-four hours a day, reciting daily the five designated prayers.

SAINTE CHAPPELLE *Paris, France*

We are reminded that God in His infinite wisdom has His own loving ways to answer our prayers.

I learned the importance of prayer in the darkest days of the Partition of India in 1947. As a child of seven, I witnessed ethnic cleansing and the worst crimes against humanity on both sides of the border of India and Pakistan. Millions of lives were devastated in that religious madness. I survived the fateful days of September 1947 to share with you that God heard our prayers and took all our family to safety when over a million people lost their lives. I have no explanation for my incredible good fortune except that prayers and faith sustained and saved us. Prayer continues to guide my life each day.

We are all witness to the power of prayer. Prayer works more miracles than we can possibly imagine. We often hear of angelic spirits responding to prayers and bringing hope, healing, and renewal of broken spirits in the middle of despair, uncertainty, and tragedy.

Prayer is a matter of conscience. It is an expression of our deepest emotions as they relate to our faith tradition. Prayer is a sacred human right, a cherished freedom, which must be safeguarded as long as it does not infringe upon the rights of others. For a believer, faith is strength, sustenance, and life, and a sacred part of his/her very being. Prayer is our direct communication with the Creator. Nothing could be more fundamental.

STS. PETER AND PAUL CATHEDRAL

Archdiocese of Indianapolis
The Catholic Church in Indiana
(1834 - 1984)

SS. PETER & PAUL CATHEDRAL *Indianapolis, Indiana*

"SO THEN, YOU ARE NO LONGER STRANGERS AND SOJOURNERS, BUT FELLOW CITIZENS WITH THE SAINTS AND MEMBERS OF THE HOUSEHOLD OF GOD, BUILT UPON THE FOUNDATION OF THE APOSTLES AND PROPHETS, CHRIST JESUS HIMSELF BEING THE CHIEF CORNERSTONE".
— EPHESIANS 2:19-20

THE PEOPLE OF BROADWAY UNITED METHODIST CHURCH HAVE WORSHIPPED IN THE MAGNIFICENT GOTHIC STRUCTURE AT THE CORNER OF FALL CREEK PARKWAY AND 29TH STREET SINCE 1927. ON THREE OCCASIONS, BROADWAY CHURCH HAS PLACED ENGRAVED CORNERSTONES AT THE JUNCTURES OF THE PRESENT COMPLEX: FOR THE SANCTUARY AREA (1925 - HERBERT FOLTZ, ARCHITECT), THE CHAPEL / PARLOR (1952 - MC GUIRE & SHOOK, ARCHITECTS), AND THE EDUCATION FACILITY (1964 - MC GUIRE, SHOOK, COMPTON & RICHEY ASSOC.) EACH NEW BUILDING WAS AN EXPRESSION OF THE HOSPITALITY WHICH SOUGHT TO TRANSFORM STRANGERS INTO FELLOW CITIZENS, SOJOURNERS INTO SAINTS.

IN RECENT YEARS, THE CONGREGATION HAS ESTABLISHED STRONG NEIGHBORHOOD OUTREACH PROGRAMS IN YOUTH LEADERSHIP DEVELOPMENT, TUTORING, EMERGENCY ASSISTANCE AND HOUSING REHABILITATION.

THE BROADWAY CHURCH OF THE FUTURE CONTINUES THIS LEGACY AS A CATHEDRAL OF THE SPIRIT. OUR SPIRITUAL CORNERSTONE IS SEEN IN THE 1990 MISSION STATEMENT: " AS FOLLOWERS OF JESUS CHRIST, RESPONDING TO GOD'S LOVE, OUR VISION IS TO BE A MULTICULTURAL CHRISTIAN COMMUNITY WHO, IN ITS MINISTRY SEEKS, WELCOMES AND VALUES ALL PEOPLE."

Broadway United Methodist Church
Indianapolis, Indiana

Kanwal Prakash Singh
© May 1990

Matters of Spirit

St. John's was designed by Dietrich A. Bohlen in 1871 in French Gothic style of architecture. The rectory was completed in 1890.

St. John's Catholic Church and Rectory
Indianapolis

St. JOHN'S CATHOLIC CHURCH *Indianapolis, Indiana*

Our spirit is a unique life-force that shapes our understanding and responses to the complex spectrum of human concerns, conditions, and challenges. It is a deep inner voice, a subconscious energy that gives word and image to our daily encounters with life. Our spirit may reveal our insights, character, and strength and define our true nature as human beings.

Matters of spirit affirm our universal human origin. We know and witness that humanity has many shared beliefs, interests, pursuits, and traditions.

Matters of spirit are best served where there is freedom of thought and action. Freedom is the life-breath of the spirit. We must recognize and respect the individuality and unique rhythms that are an integral part of our fellow human beings. Our spirit is shaped and enriched by many diverse factors: history, geography, culture, society, community, and experiences. Each element leaves its own significant impressions and impact on our spirit. For our spirit to flourish, we must assure precious freedoms as important basic rights.

Matters of spirit demand that we embrace diversity in its many forms: diversity of origin, ideas, culture, traditions, identity, perceptions, and perspectives. We must approach all matters with great cultural sensitivity, breadth of vision, and generosity of spirit. We must be willing to understand and appreciate the interests and approaches different from our own. We must treat all living beings with the respect and dignity that they deserve. Many dimensions of the human spirit-anger, sadness, generosity, compassion, selfishness, passion- meet us at the crossroads of life. An all-embracing spirit can be a "bridge" across our many differences and divides. Our focus must be to find common threads and promote unity. We know that the same hopes and dreams excite many of us.

Matters of spirit must focus on the future with hope. We must build our trust and spirit by exploring new dimensions and directions that help dispel the darkness of the past. A healthy spirit is vital to experience the fullness of life.

Matters of spirit must be encouraged to enlarge our human potential. Bringing hope and healing to others must always be an important component of our personal endeavors. The absence of this worthy commitment diminishes our spirit and our humanity.

This beautiful church in Gothic Revival style in 1886 replaced the original
church founded in 1710. It is the second oldest Catholic church with a contin-
-uous record in the United States. Designed in the basic cruciform
plan, the Church includes the twin spires, common in northern
French churches. The Church's history is interlocked with the history of
Detroit.

Ste. Anne de Detroit
Detroit, Michigan

Kanwar Prakash Singh
© 2003

STE. ANNE DE DETROIT *Detroit, Michigan*

87

Matters of spirit may be compared to a diamond in the rough. Each has many facets and awesome hidden beauty waiting to be discovered. There is a possibility that we may be rewarded with a brilliant masterpiece. Matters of spirit prepare us for unexpected turns in destiny. We must always orient our spirit toward the Light and align it with the rays of sunshine, seasons of Hope, spirit of Faith, and elements of positive energy. Then we must let time and life work their own miracles in our future.

All matters of spirit, life, and human destiny are ultimately in the Hands of God. We must simply nurture life with our hearts, with the right spirit, and all our gifts. We must add Faith and Prayer to our efforts. Prayer has its own miracles for our journey.

Matters of spirit are about selfless service. They are not just about our needs, demands, and expectations. They are about the triumph of Life itself and honoring our Creator. It cannot be just a coincidence that all faith traditions have commandments about Seva (selfless service), claiming that Seva bestows understanding, steadiness, and radiance to our spirit. We endlessly seek God's blessings to illuminate our path, show us the Way, lead us past the darkness, cleanse our spirit, and free us from the endless "circles" of Transmigration. Divine Messengers have revealed that the passage to the ultimate reunion with the Supreme Creator lies through Simran (meditation and remembrance of His Name) and tireless Seva.

We know, having unsuccessfully tried and tested our own willful ways for the past several million years, that God alone holds the final promise for all of us. We have to walk toward our future with humility, a trusting spirit, and in the Light. As one who believes in Transmigration, I may as well remember that there may be many lifetimes ahead until I get it right.

ST. MARY'S CATHOLIC CHURCH *Indianapolis, Indiana*

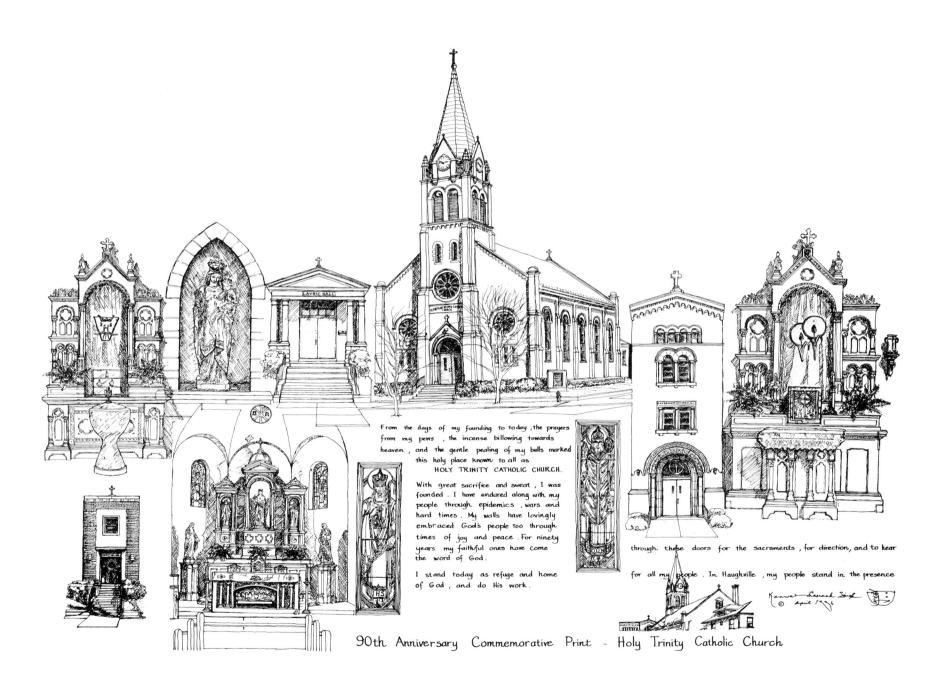

From the days of my founding to today, the prayers
from my pews, the incense billowing towards
heaven, and the gentle pealing of my bells marked
this holy place known to all as
HOLY TRINITY CATHOLIC CHURCH.

With great sacrifice and sweat, I was
founded. I have endured along with my
people through epidemics, wars and
hard times. My walls have lovingly
embraced God's people too through
times of joy and peace. For ninety
years my faithful ones have come
the word of God.

I stand today as refuge and home
of God, and do His work.

through these doors for the sacraments, for direction, and to hear

for all my people. In Haughville, my people stand in the presence

90th Anniversary Commemorative Print - Holy Trinity Catholic Church

ST. PAUL'S WAS FOUNDED IN 1866 AND ONCE SERVED AS THE CATHEDRAL FOR THE DIOCESE OF INDIANAPOLIS. IT WAS MOVED FROM THE CORNER OF NEW YORK AND ILLINOIS STREETS TO 61ST. AND NORTH MERIDIAN STREET IN 1946.

St. Paul's Episcopal Church
Indianapolis, Indiana

January 1985

St. Paul's Episcopal Church *Indianapolis, Indiana*

St. Louis Cathedral, located in the historic French Quarter of New Orleans (also known as the "Crescent City" founded on the bend of Mississippi River in 1718), is the oldest continuously active Roman Catholic Cathedral in the United States. Originally built in 1724, the present church overlooks beautiful Jackson Square and was dedicated in 1794.

St. Louis Cathedral
New Orleans, Louisiana

Kanwar Prakash Singh
© 2003

Majestic 'Mansions' of Faiths

Sacred architecture offers reflections of the divine and high achievements in building and the arts. Majestic "mansions" of faiths, some located in the grand cathedrals of nature, on ocean fronts, mountain tops, and by lakes, transport the spirit high above temporal distractions. Each cathedral, rich in history, tradition, architectural style, and spirit, inspires images and sentiments of a higher realm.

Inside a sacred place, one may experience an aura that is unique to a faith: worship traditions, music, symbols and ceremonies for reflection, prayer and communion with the sacred. All enshrine cultural and artistic treasures and provide a window to the sacred and celestial. The sanctity of these cathedrals cannot be measured in temporal terms. They represent divine wisdom and inspire deep emotions.

Ask a Sikh about the Golden Temple at Amritsar, the holiest shrine of the Sikh faith. Under the "majestic domes" of the Golden Temple reverberates an unmistakable message of unity, tolerance, service, dignity of all people, and sovereignty of all faiths.

Ask a Jew about the Wailing Wall in Jerusalem that evokes the memory of Jewish faith, history, struggle, and sacrifice. Ask a Catholic about St. Peter's and the Vatican, which enshrine the sacred heritage and spiritual treasures of his faith. Ask a Muslim about the sacred Haj at Mecca and a visit to the grand Mosque, an experience of a lifetime with promise of rewards in the afterlife.

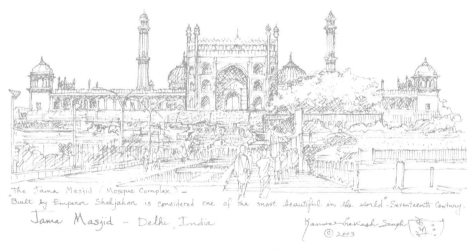

JAMA MASJID *Delhi, India*

Ask a Hindu about the sacred places of pilgrimage and their intimate associations with the pantheon of gods and goddesses.

Ask a Buddhist about the sacred sites in Tibet, India, and across Asia and sense his pride, devotion, and anguish. Ask an American Indian about the sacred cathedrals of nature that inspire, nurture, and capture his soul. There are countless other faith communities with temples providing spiritual anchors for their followers.

Divine messengers and followers of other faiths have left their imprints on our sacred places. Today, visitors come in peace to worship or enjoy these beautiful sites and hallowed grounds.

Since its founding in 1588, the Sikh Golden Temple has been desecrated repeatedly by conquering armies, religious fanatics and bigots, and unjust rulers. Each outrage that robs one faith of its priceless heritage denies us important divine wisdom. Each injury to the sentiments of the followers of one faith is an affront to human dignity of all peace-loving souls.

It is our collective responsibility to safeguard the sanctity of all sacred places and build bridges of trust and mutual respect among faith communities. Every sacred relic, edifice, church, synagogue, site, sanctuary, expression, and historic tradition must be protected as the cultural and sacred trust of mankind.

ISRAEL COMPOSITE

Music, Life, and Spirit

usic is one of the most precious gifts to the human spirit. Music is the language of gods and celestial beings and the universal language of man. It signals cosmic dimensions and unmistakable imprints of both the celestial and earthly realms.

Music is a powerful force in human affairs. As a language of the heart and soul, music transcends all divides, boundaries of culture, ethnicity, language, and faith traditions. Music can embrace and unite the whole world in its warmth and divine magic. Music can, and does, set the whole world dancing.

As a creative form, music has no equal. It can express the innermost thoughts and feelings, fantastic images, and deep emotions in the simplest of notes. It can touch the core of our being. Man has sought comfort, healing, love, pleasure, courage, and strength in music. Man has also expressed his pain, suffering, loss, and anguish with music. Man has celebrated and honored the living and dead with song and music. In music, man has found a friend and an exalted experience.

Magnificent music halls, serene and sacred architectural spaces, and nature's breath-taking "cathedrals" can add their own aura and mystique to magnify our experience of music. A superb performer can create the magic of music anywhere.

Many sacred scriptures remind us that the earth and heavens reverberate with music and song at all times; "God's Heavenly Mansion resounds with

ST. JOAN OF ARC CATHOLIC CHURCH *Indianapolis, Indiana*

offerings of music by noble saints, warriors, celestial beauties, and countless others" (Sikh scriptures). On Earth, we hear music in the rustling of leaves, gurgling of streams, songs of birds, falling rain, and the laughter of all living beings. Man creates music for the celebration of life, in countless ways and with musical instruments, vocal styles, patterns, and rhythms. We are moved by the strains of "Amazing Grace," the haunting sound of Scottish bagpipes, and the royal and rich sounds of the Indian sarod (a string instrument much like a sitar) recalling images and echoes of the Mogul royal court.

Our mind and spirit can sometimes experience a special kind of music even in the midst of silence. We "hear" music in our soul when we witness beautiful sights: golden sunsets, rising crescent of the moon, natural and man-made wonders. Our mind resounds with the "sound" of awe and wonder, when we see the snow-covered peaks, sacred cathedrals, and the cosmic dance of light in the sky. The twinkling stars strung across the heavens, a carpet of lotus flowers on a murky Indian pond, a bird in flight, a lone raindrop, and countless other silent images all sing to us. In the stillness of the night, we are sometimes "visited" by our special memories of the secret encounters with our loved ones, past life experiences, unfolding events, and future dreams. They may invite a whole new spectrum of enthralling "musical echoes" that may be hard to define or describe.

Cathédrale de Nôtre-Dame is a masterpiece of Gothic architecture. The construction of the famous Cathedral began in 1163 AD and completed in 1345 AD. The Cathedral is a "vast symphony of stone" and stands on the Ile de La Cité, and is the symbolic heart of the city of Paris.

Notre-Dame Cathedral
Paris, France

Kanwal Prakash Singh
© 2003

In most faith traditions, music plays a central role in religious worship, festivals, celebrations, and ceremonies. We celebrate the Divine and offer praise to the Supreme Creator with music: songs, prayers, sacred hymns and chants in a diversity of languages, styles, and musical instruments. Some worship traditions also include other lively arts, such as dance and drama. In sacred hymns, we see images of the Divine; with music, we touch and honor the Divine.

Man's deep attraction and relationship with music is ancient and inspired by some subconscious, invisible supernatural force and spiritual recollections. Music has origins in the Divine at one end and temporal inspirations at the other end. Great musicians understand and experience this cosmic connection and the power of music in human affairs. A well-designed space and dignified environment are essential to create and experience the full richness of sacred and classical music. Music halls, opera houses, and sacred spaces testify to the special design considerations for music.

Recognizing music as a divine gift, musicians have dedicated this art form to uplifting human spirit, sight, and imagination to the unseen horizons and touching the deepest sanctums of our soul. In music, we have found the common threads that bind cultures, traditions, emotions, and people to each other. We are awed by the splendor and mystery of nature and creation. We acknowledge and express our excitement and devotion with music.

Music, in its purest form, is the life-breath of the spirit. It affirms the unity of the human spirit. There is a universal yearning to honor and celebrate the divine within music, and through music we imagine and discover the Divine. In music we seek and find peace, inspiration, and renewal. With music, as our common "bridge," we can find new friends on the other side and everywhere.

"OLD CATHERAL" ST. FRANCIS XAVIER CHURCH

Archdiocese of Indianapolis
The Catholic Church in Indiana
(1834 - 1984)

ST. FRANCIS XAVIER CHURCH Vincennes, Indiana

The Duomo -
Como , Italy

Kanwal Prakash Singh
April 1988

THE DUOMO *Como, Italy*

97

A Pilgrimage Beyond the Glaciers

No walls other than your faith and a steady spirit separate you from the dizzying heights and depths. The entire mountain climb above 10,000 feet is along a narrow footpath hewn through solid rock towering to great heights on one side and overlooking gorgeous valleys thousands of feet below on the other side.

Along with hundreds of pilgrims, I crossed the two glaciers a kilometer apart at about 13,000 feet. Fresh steps are cut in the passageways through the glaciers each morning for the pilgrims to continue their climb to Hemkunt Sahib, located deep in the Himalayas. The walls of ice through the glaciers are seven or eight feet tall. The thought crosses my mind: what if the thin passageways cut in the mighty glacier closed in, and I am forever frozen in ice and time? I immediately dismiss such thoughts. I remember that I am on a journey of faith.

The climb beyond the glaciers tests one's physical endurance. The last 1,400 steps cut and chiseled in rock and boulders take me to the top at a height of 15, 210 feet. A historic Sikh shrine is located here. As I climb the last step, a frozen landscape and hundreds of pilgrims in bright yellow turbans greet me. From a distance, their turbans appear as marigold flowers scattered across the white snow-covered landscape. Much of the temple, in the shape of an inverted lotus-flower, is buried under snow. In front of the shrine, there is a natural lake fed by a glacier and melting snow. The faithful take the ritual bath in the frozen lake before entering the temple. The mountain, ringing and hugging the lake, rises to over 17, 500 feet, and seven snow-covered peaks (Sapat Sring) form a crown at the top. The beauty of the place is beyond description. When I look up, the sky is deep pure blue and the heavens much closer.

The frozen lake, almost two miles in circumference, is the source of Hem Ganga, a tributary of the Ganges River. Directly behind, the massive, snow-covered Somair Purbut (mountain) is glistening in the afternoon sun. From this Himalayan perch, we see a deep and vast valley, hills and glaciers, and carpets of clouds thousands of feet below. The troubles of the temporal world are a million miles away. I feel a divine presence. The spirit and sacred relics of the great Sikh Guru, who meditated here in a previous life, are all around. Pilgrims make return visits to this unique place in the Valley of Gods. I am overwhelmed with emotion to make my first spiritual pilgrimage with my brother and sister to this hallowed place.

"Cathedrals of Spirit"

Silent Reflections

In my silent reflections, I often ask God:

"How much farther lies Your destination for my life?
My heart yearns to see Your Sacred Footprint.
I long to witness Your Presence around me,
Pray that You know and witness my burdens."

I imagine God's response:

"Do not pause!
Just know that I am here,
For, I am the Thought, the Spirit, and the Life,
The Word, the Witness, and the Destiny.
I am enshrined in every rhythm and living fiber,
Manifested in every Temporal and Celestial Realm.
I am the Sound, the Silence, the Wonder, and the Light.
I am in all your imaginings, blessings, and endeavors,
I am; I was in every trial and triumph
Along your passage through many lifetimes.
I will always be with all that I have Created."

"Go forward in Faith and Prayer!
With a humble heart and an inspired spirit:
Serve with all the gifts entrusted unto you,
Radiate friendliness, share and seek peace,
Cherish the Promise of Life,
Help others with their dreams.
I will carry your burdens and walk the distance."

I am awakened to witness His Divine Presence, Imprints, and Blessings all around.

Dukh Bhanjani at Golden Temple, Amritsar, India
17th Century A.D.

Sanwar P. Singh
January 1984

DUKH BHANJANI AT GOLDEN TEMPLE *Amritsar, India*

GOLDEN TEMPLE,

Gilded Panel, Amritsar, India

ART *in* ARCHITECTURE

WE EMPLOY A spectrum of design, structural, decorative, and other fine arts to create buildings that are superb examples of architecture. Many historic monuments and landmarks stand as testimony to this endeavor.

In the interiors of such edifices, we find breathtaking columns, sculptures, wall treatments, domed and vaulted ceilings, rich design elements, stained-glass windows and skylights, chandeliers, tapestries, paintings, and other furnishings successfully integrated into the design of the space. There is a beautiful dance of light, color, decorations, and artistic surprises for the eyes, mind, and spirit. The exteriors capture our imagination with magnificent entrances, niches with statues of gods and saints, carved

THE BRONZE STATUE GROUP, REPRESENTING LITERATURE, SCIENCE AND ARTS WAS CREATED BY RICHARD W. BOCK OF ILLINOIS, WHO BEGAN HIS CAREER IN 1880'S WORKING WITH FRANK LLOYD WRIGHT AND OTHER ARCHITECTS INVOLVED IN THE PRAIRIE SCHOOL. THE STATUE GROUP ADORNED THE INDIANAPOLIS PUBLIC LIBRARY FROM 1892 TO 1967 AT 150 NORTH MERIDIAN STREET. IN 1981 THE STATUE WAS PERMANENTLY INSTALLED AT CENTRAL LIBRARY WHERE THE SPIRIT OF KNOWLEDGE IS EMBODIED IN MORE THAN A MILLION BOOKS.

"Literature, Science and Arts" Statue - Central Library
Indianapolis Marion County Public Library

INDIANAPOLIS MARION COUNTY LIBRARY *Indianapolis, Indiana*

and inlayed floors and facades, and the use of a variety of materials and techniques. The buildings may proudly display architectural highlights: impressive towers, spires and steeples, shining domes, and other distinguishing features that add dignity, identity, and artistic charm to the architecture. The transitional and immediate space leading to the structure may offer other special details in the form of pavement patterns, sculptures, fountains, reflecting pools, and imaginative lighting and landscape in the courtyard.

Our fascination with art has inspired us to create temples out of solid rock (Ajanta and Ellora Caves, India), paint walls and entire ceilings with frescoes (Sistine Chapel, Vatican), and build structures that resemble ancient chariots (Sun Temple, Konarak, India). Imagine embellishing the immense facades with three million giant sculptures with mythological inspiration (Meenakashi Temple, Madurai, India), the brilliant craftsmanship of the Blue Mosque, Istanbul, Turkey, and creating the legendary European castles, palaces, and gardens.

The drawings in this section include a few examples of art gracing and enhancing architecture and our urban environment. We see in nature and our imagination the source of these inspirations. We interpret and imitate these images to fulfill our creative urges and to discover our true spirit that finds resonance in art. The accompanying text offers reflections on the place, presence, and spirit of art in life, nature, and architecture.

ANCIENT TEMPLE *Khujaraho, India*

Blackburne
Apartment - 1896
[Romanesque
influence]

Second
Presbyterian
church - 1888
[arches]

St. Paul E. Church - 1941

Crown Hill Walk and
Waiting Station - 1885
[Gothic Revival]

UNION STATION
UNION STATION
[Romanesque
Revival]

Federal
Building
1905
[Neo-classic
Doric
Column]

1930 [The Art Deco - Egyptian influence]

CIRCLE TOWER

MURAT
Murat
Temple - 1910
[middle east
architecture
and motif]

State House - 1888
[classical Corinthian style]

Indianapolis
Athletic
Club - 1923
[Italian
Renaissance]

Old Athletic
Club
1907
[Florentine
Renaissance]

Wilking Music Co - 1872
[Italianate]

Maennerchor Building - 1906 [demolished 1975]
[South German architectural tradition]

Doorways, windows and
arches are vital architectural
elements which lead
the observer into and allow him to look
out of any building or space.

Embellished with floral designs,
geometrical and abstract patterns,
animal and human figures, as
well as stylized identification
signs and ornamentations in
a variety of building materials,
they reflect the inspirations, ideas,
history and heritage that went
into the shaping of the total structure.

Indianapolis IV
[Doorways and Windows]

Indiana Theatre - 1927
[Indian and Egyptian
influence]

Federal Building
1905
[Neo-classic]

The Majestic
Building -
1895

Gate, Indianapolis Museum
of Art grounds

Athenaeum 1893-97
[German - Austrian Hapsburg mode]

Kanwal A. Singh
August 1976

Indianapolis has a rich collection of
unusual and attractive doorways and windows as an integral part of
many surviving historic - Gothic, neo-classic, Renaissance - revival,
Italianate & Victorian - structures. Other architectural traditions and
influences are also represented and add visual excitement to our city.

The Artist in Us

A rich spectrum of ideas, images, dreams, and mysterious cosmic rhythms dance inside every living being. Inspirations often motivate our spirits to express emotions, reflections, and inner urges in artistic and creative endeavors.

Some of the greatest treasures of art have emerged from our deep

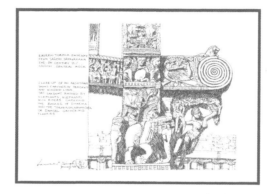

EASTERN TORANA GATEWAY *Sanchi, India*

explain the universal presence, generous adaptations, and the intense relationship of many art forms in our architecture, sacred traditions, and everyday life.

Fascinated by the power, magic, mystery, and beauty of our existence, man showcases and integrates the celebrated motifs from nature and life in

reflections, stimulated imagination, and visual meditations. Meditation opens the inner sanctum of our soul and offers us glimpses of our celestial origins and connections. Our visual meditation is a natural response to understanding and symbolically interpreting what our inner eyes see and imagine. We fashion works of art in colorful richness and diversity, and this, in part, may many forms of human creativity. At one end, art seems a bridge to unseen mysterious realms, and at the other end, art transports our spirits to the unimagined splendor of the world around us.

Mutual admiration and imitations of life and art are a well-recognized fact. It is an affirmation of the artist in each one of us and our instinctive attraction to art.

LADIES FIGURES
REPRESENT:
STATUE
LOOKING
TOWARD:
1. ASIA
2. AFRICA
3. EUROPE
AND
4. JUSTICE

PEOPLE OF THE
FORM A MORE PER

UNITED STATES,
FECT UNION...

FIRST SKYSCRAPER.

JOHN AND EVALINE HOLLIDAY GAVE THE 80 ACRE TRACT OF LAND ALONG WHITE RIVER TO THE
CITY OF INDIANAPOLIS ON DECEMBER 12, 1916 "TO BE USED AS A PLACE OF RECREATION AND THE
STUDY OF NATURE".
IN 1978 THE MASTER PLAN FOR THE PARK, DESIGNED BY INDIANAPOLIS ARTIST ELMER E. TAFLINGER,
WAS FINALLY IMPLEMENTED BRINGING ABOUT A MAJOR TRANSFORMATION AND RENOVATION OF HOLLIDAY
PARK. THE "RUINS", BUILT AROUND THREE IMMENSE STATUES, REPRESENTING THE THREE RACES OF
MAN - A NEGRO, A CAUCASIAN AND AN ORIENTAL - WITH ITS REFLECTING POOL AND FOUNTAINS
ADD A UNIQUE SETTING FOR SOME OF OUR NATION'S PAST HERITAGE. THE "RACES OF MAN"
STATUES, SCULPTED BY KARL BITTER, ONE OF AMERICA'S FOREMOST SCULPTORS, ORIGINALLY
FORMED THE FACADE OF THE OLD ST. PAUL BUILDING IN NEW YORK, AT ONE TIME THE WORLD'S
THE BEAUTIFUL STATUES OF LADIES WHICH FLANK THE "CENTERPIECE" OF "RUINS" CAME FROM THE THE OLD MARION COUNTY   COURTHOUSE DESIGNED BY
ISSAC HODGSON WHO EMPLOYED MANY FAMOUS EUROPEAN SKILLED CRAFTSMEN AND SCULPTORS TO COMPLETE THE SECOND EMPIRE STYLE ARCHITECTURAL LANDMARK IN 1876.

Holliday Park, Indianapolis

Samuel P. Singh
august 1982

Our creative pursuits fulfill an important inner need. With artistic talents, we explore and express ideas, passions, and embraced ideals, and spread and communicate knowledge and information about our special world. Through art, we touch the deeper self within and attempt to mirror its inspirations on the "canvas" of life for personal pleasure. We invite and welcome a response from others to our creative adventures.

In art and through art, we find echoes of our many shared interests. In art, we witness the dance of the temporal and celestial in "living color." Art seems to transcend the boundaries of time, life, and culture. Art offers common threads that enrich our individual and collective uniqueness. Great art belongs to the generations. A rich artistic heritage reflects and enshrines our history and journey as a civilization. Some of the greatest treasures grace and beautify magnificent architecture.

Art is much more than lines on paper or a riot of color on a canvas. Art is Life. Art has its own corner in our heart and soul. Art will continue to be a teacher, an inspiration, and a source of personal adventure in times to come. Much like the art patrons and benefactors of the past, we too must preserve and support art and artistic treasures as our legacy to the future. The human spirit will always seek new inspirations. Man continues to enjoy the creative gifts of Shakespeare, Leonardo Da Vinci, Michelangelo, Vincent Van Gogh, Picasso, Chagall, Henry Moore, and other giants who left their

TREVI FOUNTAIN *Rome, Italy*

St. Mark's Basilica   Venice, Italy
11th-16th Cent.   Venetian Byzantine Style

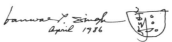

Sanwar Singh
April 1986

THE INDIANA THEATRE *Indianapolis, Indiana*

imprints and signatures on our artistic legacy. We are mindful of their sacrifice and genius. Some of their works transform us, while others continue to leave us speechless in wonder.

We must commit ourselves to educating future generations about the importance of the arts, especially in this era of expanding technology, maddening pace of life, and many competing interests. We must strengthen the idea that art can be a life-saving refuge, teacher, and friend. Communities and institutions must vigorously introduce the arts to the young and assure its place in their future. Let us awaken and encourage the artist within. Art is part of our humanity; it can soften the noises and distractions that make us so restless today. Let us channel needed resources to this effort. Let us anticipate and make room for the creative endeavors, visions, and surprises of the great geniuses and masters of the future.

यह पत्थर की दीवार दक्षि-
णी भारत के मैसूर प्रांत में
बैलूर शहर के चिन्नकेसवा
मन्दिर पर है॥ यह मन्दिर
बाहरवीं सदी ईसवी में होय-
साला राजों ने बनवाये॥
यह मन्दिर अति सुन्दर बुत-
कारी के लिए प्रसिद्ध हैं॥
इस मन्दिर की बाहरली और
भीतरी दीवारों और थम्मों पर
हिन्दू देवी, देवताओं और
अप्सराओं और होयसाला
राजों के दरबार, लड़ाईयों
और कारनामों की मूरतियां हैं॥

THIS BEAUTIFULLY SCULPTUR-
ED WALL IS A PART OF THE
CHENNAKESAVA TEMPLE AT
BELUR IN MYSORE STATE, SOUTH
INDIA. THESE TEMPLES WHICH DA-
TE FROM TWELFTH CENTURY AD
WERE BUILT BY HOYSALA KINGS.
THESE TEMPLES ARE FAMOUS
FOR THEIR EXQUISITE CARVINGS
ON THE EXTERIOR AND INTERIOR WA-
LLS AND COLUMNS-BEAUTIFULLY CHI-
SELLED-WHICH SUPPORT
THE STRUCTURE. THESE SCUL-
PTURES PRESENT A PANORAMA
OF HINDU GODS, GODDESSES
AND SCENES FROM THE COURT
AND REIGN OF THE HOYSALA KINGS

Chennakesava Temple, Belur (MYSORE STATE), India

Kanwar Prakash Singh
© 1972

CHENNAKESAVA TEMPLE *Belur, India*

Mosaic of Light

There was just a hint of light on the distant horizon. Past the valleys of dark clouds stretched in front, one could see a scarlet glow in the distance heralding an approaching dawn. The sun was still below the horizon., and the earth was dark, catching the last few moments of rest before the arrival of another day.

The city of Miami, Florida, was all lit-up as our flight from Buenos Aires, Argentina, approached for landing. From the air, Miami seemed like a gigantic mosaic of lights: clusters, webs, squares, and strings of light stretching for miles in several directions. Beyond the magic of lights, we could imagine that the city was home and crossroads to many lives and cultures.

Aerial imagery and night visuals have added another dimension to urban design in today's cityscape. This has not been lost sight of as a powerful creative opportunity. The lights and illuminations at night lend a festive aura and highlights to the landscape. They add fascination, mystery, and sensuous pleasure at the pedestrian level.

Besides the visual impressions, creative adaptation of lights offers an engraved invitation to come and discover much more. The midnight magic in Times Square on New Year's Eve, colorful billboards of the Ginza district in Tokyo, and the serene illuminations for Diwali at the Golden Temple of Amritsar, flashed across my mind. (Many remember the recent dazzling millennium lighting and fireworks show at Sydney Harbor, the Eiffel Tower in Paris, and other world capitals). Each renewed their invitation to visit.

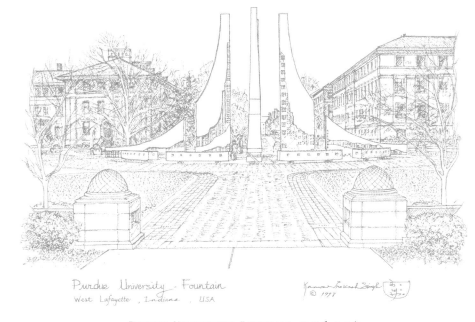

Purdue University - Fountain
West Lafayette, Indiana, USA

Kanwar Trilochan Singh
© 1998

PURDUE UNIVERSITY FOUNTAIN *West Lafayette, Indiana*

Monument Circle has identified Indianapolis to the rest of the nation since Alexander Ralston designed the original plan for the city in 1821. To tradition minded Hoosiers, their majestic centerpiece – the towering Soldiers and Sailors Monument – symbolizes a landmark that evokes many emotions.

Monument Circle underwent major renovation in 1978. The pavement patterns, the new lighting fixtures and the carefully planned landscaping have greatly enhanced the beauty of the monument designed by Bruno Schmitz of Berlin, Germany and dedicated in 1902. The sculptures at the base of the monument were completed by Rudolph Schwarz of Germany. The present Columbia Club, in English Mansard style was designed by Rubush and Hunter of Indianapolis and completed in 1925. Christ Church Cathedral, designed by William Tinsley of England, has adorned the heart of the city since 1860.

Monument Circle III

Samuel P. Singh
March 1982

ਇਹ ਬੁਤਕਾਰੀ ਦੀ ਮਿਸਾਲ
ਬਾਰਵੀਂ ਸਦੀ ਦੀ ਹੋਇਸਾ-
ਰਾਜ ਮੰਦਰ ਤੇ ਮੌਜੂਦ ਹੈ॥

ਇਹ ਮੰਦਰ ਦਖਣੀ ਭਾਰਤ
ਦੇ ਹੈਲੇਬਿਡ ਸ਼ਹਿਰ ਜਿਸ
ਨੂੰ ਪੁਰਾਣੇ ਵਕਤਾਂ ਵਿਚ ਦੋਰਾ-
ਸਮੂਦਰਾ ਦੀ ਕਹਿੰਦੇ ਸਨ,
ਹੋਇਸਾਲਾ ਰਾਜਿਆਂ ਦੀ
ਪੁਰਾਣੀ ਰਾਜਧਾਨੀ ਸੀ॥

ਇਸ ਮੰਦਰ ਦੀਆਂ ਬਾਹਰੀ-
ਆਂ ਕੰਧਾਂ ਤੇ ਇੰਨ੍ਹੇ ਸਾਰੇ ਬ-
ਹੀ ਹਿੰਦੂ ਦੇਵੀਆਂ ਅਤੇ ਦੇ-
ਵਤਿਆਂ ਦੇ ਬੁਤ ਹਨ॥ਇ-
ਸ ਬੁਤ ਵਿਚ ਵਿਸ਼ਨੂ ਨਰਸਿੰ-
ਘ ਦੇ ਰੂਪ ਵਿਚ ਆਪਣੇ
ਦੁਸ਼ਮਣ ਹਰਨਾਕਿਸ਼ਪੁ
ਦਾ ਨਾਸ਼ ਕਰ ਰਿਹਾ ਹੈ॥

THIS MARVELLOUS EX-
AMPLE OF SCULPTOR'
S ART EXISTS ON THE
HOYASALESWARA
TEMPLE OF 12TH.
CENTURY A.D. THIS
TEMPLE IS LOCATED
IN THE SOUTH INDIA-
N CITY OF HALEBID
ONCE KNOWN AS—
DARASAMUDRA,
THE ANCIENT CAPIT-
OL OF HOYASALA E-
MPIRE. THE LARGE
PANELS OF GODS
AND GODDESSES
OF THE HINDU PAN-
THEON ADORN T-
HE OUTER WALLS
OF THE TEMPLE.
IN THIS SCULP-
TURE, VISHNU
AS NARSINHA
OR LION-GOD
DESTROYS HIS
ENEMY
HIRANAYAK-
ASYPU

Hoyasaleswara Temple – 12th Century
Halebid, Mysore State, India

Kanwar Prakash Singh
© 1972

HOYASALESWARA TEMPLE *Halebid, India*

The Hilton at Monument Circle
Indianapolis, Indiana

THE HILTON ON MONUMENT CIRCLE *Indianapolis, Indiana*

A Reflection of Vision and Culture

Architecture, unlike many other areas of creativity, carries a special distinction; it embraces many disciplines. It is a repository of artistic accomplishments reflecting a spirit of adventure in building design, successfully combining form, function, and aesthetics.

Architecture reflects ethnic, cultural, and spiritual identity, as well as regional influences. Architecture combines many skills and elements to create enclosures for living, working, worshiping, learning, and celebrating, Basic architectural components—design, structure, and space—are fashioned with materials and details that best reflect the function.

Architecture expresses our societal vision to advance human promise. It has provided us a "laboratory" to understand life and to unravel the mystery of our universe. In architecture, the builders have tried to meet the demands of human purpose and promise. In architecture, one finds an impressive record of man's journey through the ages, from modest mud huts to the imposing castle.

In architecture of historic significance, we witness that many areas of human interest, survival, and advancement have successfully converged. Our mind and spirit experience a live adventure into our ancient past, the highlights of the journey in progress, and the plans and visions of the future.

WAR MEMORIAL *Indianapolis, Indiana*

Butler Univ.

Morris Butler Home

Central Christian Church

Central Avenue Church

Murat Temple

St. John's Church

City Market

First Baptist Church

Majestic towers of diverse architectural styles adorn the Indianapolis skyline and dominate many neighborhoods. Rich in detail the towers enliven the city's architectural heritage. Feb. 1974.

Tabernacle Presbyterian Church

St. Mary's Catholic Church

Union Station

Benton House

St. Joan of Arc Catholic Church

Second Presbyterian Church

Indianapolis II

5/50

Ganvant P. Singh

प्रध्ययुगीन मूर्तिकला   कँवल प्रकाश सिंह
अप्रैल १६८०

MEDIEVAL SCULPTURE *Konarek, India*

Tourists, scholars, and pilgrims in record numbers are traveling to heritage sites and famous destinations as never before. Technology, research, and travel bring us face to face with the architectural past near home and in distant lands and cultures. For some, such excursions offer surprising insights and spiritual connections, for others, new understandings and inspirations for the future.

How can society best preserve and adapt the fast-diminishing old treasures into the future urban fabric and landscape of our communities? Government and the private sector must combine forces to integrate historic architectural resources into the master plans of the world heritage sites and save them from destruction. This is truly one of the great challenges of the new millennium. Many communities around the world are embracing preservation. Nations are finding unexpected rewards in such investments.

CHENNAKESAVA TEM-
PLE, BELUR, MYSORE
STATE, SOUTH INDIA
COMPLETED IN 1117 A.D.
BY KING VISHNU
VARDHANA - VIRTUAL
FOUNDER OF HOYA-
SALA DYNASTY.
THIS TEMPLE IS THE
FINEST EXAMPLE OF
CHALUKYAN STYLE OF
ARCHITECTURE AND
IS FAMOUS FOR ITS
EXQUISITELY CARVED
WALLS, CEILING, PILLARS AND
STATUARY. ITS EXTERIOR WALLS
ARE ENRICHED BY HORIZONTAL
ANIMAL FRIEZES, SCUPTURES
OF GODS, GODDESSES AND
CELESTIAL BEAUTIES □□□

चित्रकेशवा मन्दिर, बैलूर
मैसूर प्रांत, दक्षिणी भारत-

यह मन्दिर महाराजा विशण
वरधण, जो होआसाला वंश
के स्थापतीये, ने ११७ई
में बनवाया था। यह
मन्दिर चलूकिया शिलप
वस्तु और कारीगिरी के

बहुत सुन्दर मिसाल
है॥ यह मन्दिर अति
सुन्दर दीवारों, छत
थमों और मूरतियों के
लिए प्रसिद्ध है॥ इस
मन्दिर की बाहरली दीवारों पर
जानवरों, देवी देवताओं और
सुन्दर आपसराओं की मूरतीयो
की सज्जावट है॥ □□□□□□

1973

Belur Mysore State India : Chennakesava Temple

© 1973

Silver Threads of Rain

In front of our hotel window on the twelfth floor, there was a vast stretch of open vista, interrupted only by the high-rise buildings way in the distance. Falling rain suddenly shrouded the view and the outlines of buildings. It was fascinating to see rain add an aura of mystery to the urban environment of Buenos Aires, Argentina.

The rain appeared like countless glistening threads of silver many blocks deep, rushing downward as if pulled by an invisible force below. The rain resembled threads on a weaver's giant loom. The rain-threads were being pulled and tugged by the workings of the loom. Right through this moving, glowing, and translucent screen of silver rain-threads, one could see the entire scene below: the morning traffic, streets, buildings, statues, trees, and people. I was witnessing water lend beauty and magnificence to the architecture and the environment.

The landscape and the urban air were being bathed by this heavenly gift. Intermittently, the rain became intense and soft. It was a not a threatening or disruptive rain: a welcome and refreshing rain for the city, soil, birds, winter crops, and the human spirit.

The Buddha, KamaKura, Japan
The Great Amida Buddha (Daibutsu of KamaKura)
13th Century, Bronze

THE BUDDHA *Kama Kura, Japan*

Fountain Square , Cincinnati , Ohio
TYEER DAVIDSON Fountain presented to The CITY OF CINCINNATI
by HENRY PROBASCO in 1971

Kanwar Prakash Singh
© 1994

MEENAKASHI
TEMPLE
Madurai, India

HALLS *of* LEARNING

There are thousands of well-established and recognized public and private schools, colleges, universities, and learning centers in the United States. Each institution and campus has its own unique character, history, and spirit, and the architecture often reflects the latest ideas in building.

There are many institutions of learning that serve the diverse and growing needs of the state of Indiana. Some of them are leading centers of learning, teaching, and research in the nation. In addition, several art, culture, history museums, libraries, and other centers acquaint us with the wisdom, creativity, and lifestyles of the past, and open our mind's window

UNIVERSITY OF ILLINOIS

to new ideas, inspirations, and future experiences.

The drawings in this section offer studies of several institutions of learning with a brief history of the campus, site, or complex. Defining architectural elements and attractions-including entrances, sculptures, fountains, towers, special and unusual features that best reflect the spirit, traditions, and visual character of the institutions-are highlighted and integrated into the art compositions. The text in this section relates to exploring and discovering the expanding thresholds of human experience, understanding, creativity, adventure, and spirit in the ultimate "living library" of life.

Light and Hope

Let us be a candle of Light and Hope to one another. Dispel darkness, end the cycles of violence, bring comfort and healing, and lift up the fallen and the forgotten. We can make a difference. We must break our silence about the evils, injustices, and deprivations of basic essentials needed for human survival. Let us abandon all intolerance and ignorance. Let us build bridges of knowledge, hope, and understanding and travel across them in freedom and friendship. Be kind to the environment. It nurtures our mind and spirit. Nature is the resting place and the crown of God.

Let us encourage, share, and celebrate the best in each of us. Let an enlightened spirit guide and enrich our imagination and experience. Imagine a world at peace, where children play in safety and freedom along the "seashores" of old and new frontiers. Then ask what can I do to make such a dream possible in my lifetime.

We are at crossroads in human history. Let us imagine our place on this journey. Focus on the destination. All dreams, destiny, and future hopes begin here, now, and with each one of us.

OLD MAENNERCHOR BUILDING
AT MICHIGAN AND ILLINOIS STREETS

School of Law - Indianapolis

INDIANA UNIVERSITY SCHOOL OF LAW *Indianapolis, Indiana*

STUDENT CENTER   MAXWELL HALL   BECK CHAPEL   ROSE WELL HOUSE   KIRKWOOD HALL

ART MUSEUM   MYERS HALL   WOODBURN HALL   MAIN LIBRARY

LAW SCHOOL   OWEN HALL   MUSICAL ARTS CENTER   MEMORIAL UNION   MEMORIAL STADIUM   ASSEMBLY HALL

METZ CARILLON   MUSIC HALL   SHOWALTER FOUNTAIN

"ONE OF THE OLDEST STATE UNIVERSITIES WEST OF ALLEGHENIES, INDIANA UNIVERSITY WAS FOUNDED IN 1820. THE LARGEST OF THE EIGHT CAMPUSES IS LOCATED IN BLOOMINGTON, A CITY OF ABOUT 60,000 INHABITANTS 50 MILES SOUTH OF THE STATE CAPITAL IN INDIANAPOLIS. STUDENT ENROLLMENT IN THE FIRST SEMESTER OF 1985-1986 WAS OVER 32,800.
THE 1855-ACRE BLOOMINGTON CAMPUS LIES IN SCENIC, ROLLING, HEAVILY WOODED TERRAIN IN SOUTH-ERN INDIANA .... MOST OF THE UNIVERSITY BUILDINGS ARE CONSTRUCTED OF NATIVE LIMESTONE FROM NEARBY QUARRIES.
INDIANA UNIVERSITY'S INTERNATIONAL REPUTATION FOR EXCELLENCE BRINGS STUDENTS FROM ALL 50 STATES AND 119 FOREIGN COUNTRIES. OVER 100 DEGREE PROGRAMS AND MORE THAN 5,000 COURSES ARE OFFERED IN A WIDE VARIETY OF FIELDS BY A DISTINGUISHED FACULTY AND VISITING SCHOLARS, SCIENTISTS, SPECIALISTS AND ARTISTS. IU SCHOOLS AND PROGRAMS THAT RANK AMONG THE BEST IN THE NATION INCLUDE MUSIC, OPTOMETRY, EDUCATION, BUSINESS, BOTANY, ZOOLOGY, FRENCH, ENGLISH, SPANISH, GERMAN AND RUSSIAN."

Indiana University II

May 1986

INDIANA UNIVERSITY *Bloomington, Indiana*

Making a Difference

Imagine yourself:
With courage and deep conviction
Leading a New Renaissance
Reflecting our times and spirit.

The light of your house and spirit:
Visible for miles
Across the unfamiliar and diverse landscapes
Honors all faiths, cultures, and traditions.

Your heart and home:
Offer kindness and friendship
To strangers, angels, and the newcomer;
Share sanctuary in the sunshine
Light in the darkness of the moment.

Together we can and must:
Guard against narrow divides,
Dispel ignorance, fear, and injustice;
Herald hope, healing, dreams, and dignity.
Encircle all living beings in cherished warmth and promise.

Let tomorrow's generations
Inherit this precious vision and challenge.

Each of us can lead this effort:
Share inspirations in the true spirit of faith;
Extend respect, freedom and friendship.
Make each community, culture, and wisdom next to us
Part of our common Circle of Light.

Imagine the welcome change:
Transcending cultures and frontiers,
Reaching deep into the human spirit;
A true awakening making a lasting difference.

Witness the dawn of a new day:
Right before our eyes
The birth of a new Renaissance for our times
Embracing all humanity someday
All because we dared.

University of
Michigan
is one of the
finest institution
of higher learning
in the world.
Founded in 1817 the
main campus at
Ann Arbor
is rich in
traditions and
architectural
styles. The
University attracts
students and
scholars from all
over the world
to this beautiful
campus.

University of Michigan
Ann Arbor, Michigan

UNIVERSITY OF MICHIGAN *Ann Arbor, Michigan*

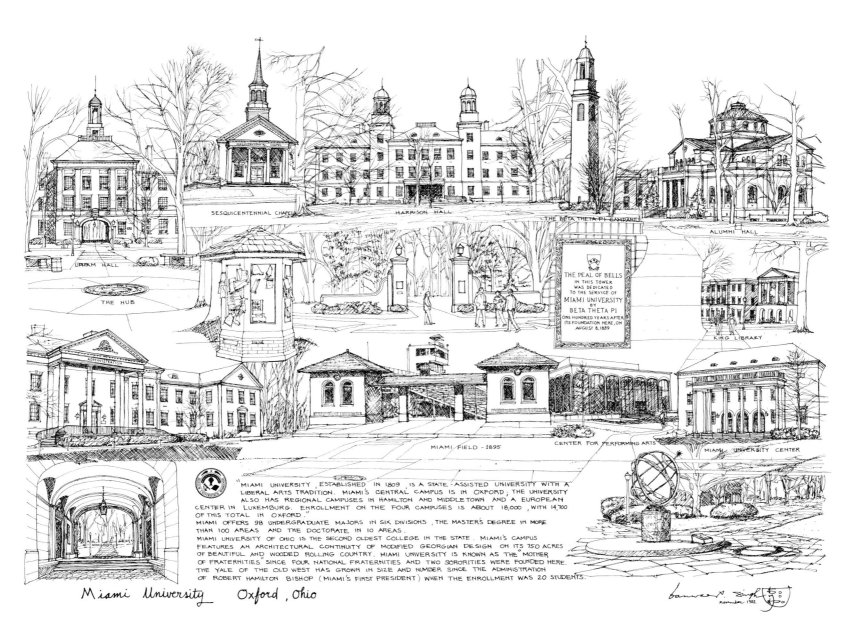

SESQUICENTENNIAL CHAPEL

HARRISON HALL

THE BETA THETA PI CAMPANILE

ALUMNI HALL

UPHAM HALL

THE HUB

THE PEAL OF BELLS
IN THIS TOWER
WAS DEDICATED
TO THE SERVICE OF
MIAMI UNIVERSITY
BY
BETA THETA PI
ONE HUNDRED YEARS AFTER
ITS FOUNDATION HERE, ON
AUGUST 8, 1839

KING LIBRARY

ADMINISTRATION

MIAMI FIELD - 1895

CENTER FOR PERFORMING ARTS

MIAMI UNIVERSITY CENTER

"MIAMI UNIVERSITY, ESTABLISHED IN 1809, IS A STATE-ASSISTED UNIVERSITY WITH A LIBERAL ARTS TRADITION. MIAMI'S CENTRAL CAMPUS IS IN OXFORD; THE UNIVERSITY ALSO HAS REGIONAL CAMPUSES IN HAMILTON AND MIDDLETOWN AND A EUROPEAN CENTER IN LUXEMBURG. ENROLLMENT ON THE FOUR CAMPUSES IS ABOUT 18,000, WITH 14,700 OF THIS TOTAL IN OXFORD."
MIAMI OFFERS 98 UNDERGRADUATE MAJORS IN SIX DIVISIONS, THE MASTER'S DEGREE IN MORE THAN 100 AREAS AND THE DOCTORATE IN 10 AREAS.
MIAMI UNIVERSITY OF OHIO IS THE SECOND OLDEST COLLEGE IN THE STATE. MIAMI'S CAMPUS FEATURES AN ARCHITECTURAL CONTINUITY OF MODIFIED GEORGIAN DESIGN ON ITS 750 ACRES OF BEAUTIFUL AND WOODED ROLLING COUNTRY. MIAMI UNIVERSITY IS KNOWN AS THE "MOTHER OF FRATERNITIES" SINCE FOUR NATIONAL FRATERNITIES AND TWO SORORITIES WERE FOUNDED HERE. THE YALE OF THE OLD WEST HAS GROWN IN SIZE AND NUMBER SINCE THE ADMINISTRATION OF ROBERT HAMILTON BISHOP (MIAMI'S FIRST PRESIDENT) WHEN THE ENROLLMENT WAS 20 STUDENTS.

Miami University   Oxford, Ohio

November 1982

Creative Inspirations

The Sikh scriptures reveal, "The Creator resides in Nature; Thy grandeur and limits beyond fathom and description." The scriptures further affirm that no one knows, "how many Indras, moons, and suns grace the mighty heavens." It is beyond human imagination and comprehension to fathom "how many stars, planets, celestial continents, clusters of heavenly bodies, and dazzling spinning galaxies are strung across the Heavens and illuminate the limitless depths and dimensions of the cosmos?"

We imagine that God is everywhere, and we are fascinated by the scripture's statement of "Nature as the resting place and Crown of God." We are drawn to the rich splendor and offerings of nature. We are awed by nature's beauty, power, magic, and mystery. We seek healing, inspirations, and renewal in nature. We search for the

Indiana University , Bloomington , Indiana

INDIANA UNIVERSITY *Bloomington, Indiana*

divine in nature. We honor the sacred with nature.

Nature holds special lessons and a universal wisdom for all creation. Nature is a limitless source to understand, enhance, and celebrate life. Man has interpreted and translated the mystery, marvels, and the beautiful designs, motifs, and symbols in nature into countless manifestations of creativity and inspiration.

For nature to surrender many of its secrets, we must first enter into harmony with life, spirit, and the universe around us. Every raindrop, sunset, bird in flight, roar of the mighty ocean, majestic landscape, wild flower, falling snowflake, and every living being carries a message and imprint of God's power and presence in all things. All around us are reflections of the Heavens and a glimpse of the Master Architect of all Creation.

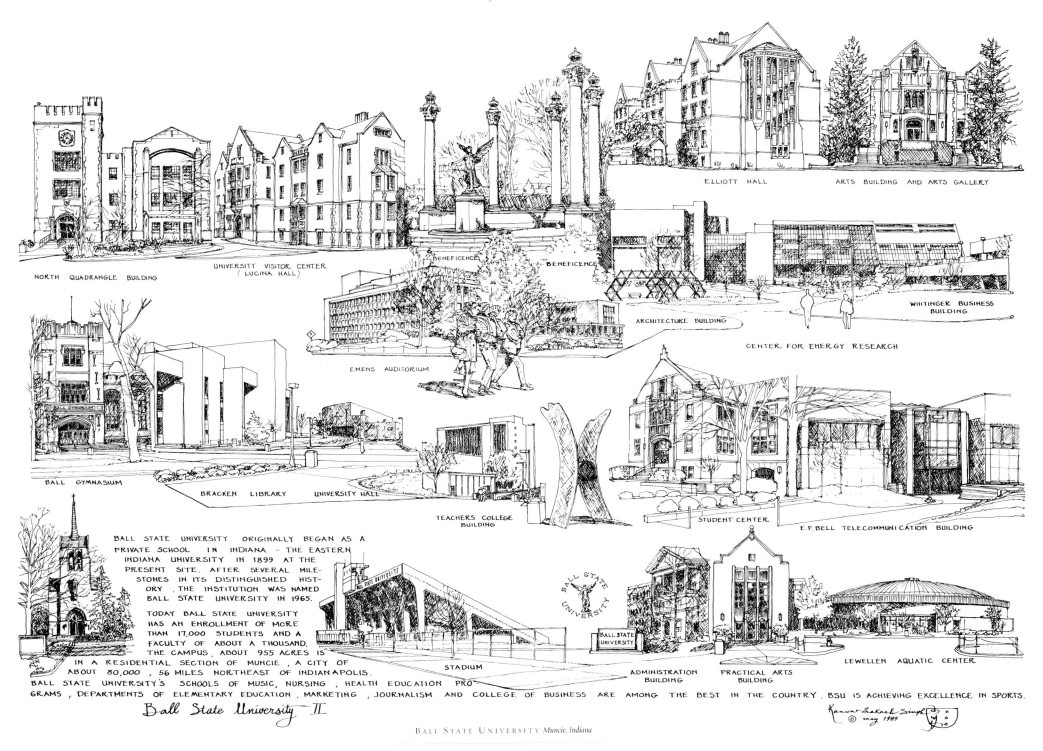

NORTH QUADRANGLE BUILDING

UNIVERSITY VISITOR CENTER
(LUCINA HALL)

BENEFICENCE

BENEFICENCE

ELLIOTT HALL

ARTS BUILDING AND ARTS GALLERY

ARCHITECTURE BUILDING

WHITINGER BUSINESS BUILDING

CENTER FOR ENERGY RESEARCH

EMENS AUDITORIUM

BALL GYMNASIUM

BRACKEN LIBRARY   UNIVERSITY HALL

TEACHERS COLLEGE BUILDING

STUDENT CENTER

E.F. BELL TELECOMMUNICATION BUILDING

BALL STATE UNIVERSITY ORIGINALLY BEGAN AS A PRIVATE SCHOOL IN INDIANA - THE EASTERN INDIANA UNIVERSITY IN 1899 AT THE PRESENT SITE. AFTER SEVERAL MILESTONES IN ITS DISTINGUISHED HISTORY, THE INSTITUTION WAS NAMED BALL STATE UNIVERSITY IN 1965.

TODAY BALL STATE UNIVERSITY HAS AN ENROLLMENT OF MORE THAN 17,000 STUDENTS AND A FACULTY OF ABOUT A THOUSAND. THE CAMPUS, ABOUT 955 ACRES IS IN A RESIDENTIAL SECTION OF MUNCIE, A CITY OF ABOUT 80,000, 56 MILES NORTHEAST OF INDIANAPOLIS. BALL STATE UNIVERSITY'S SCHOOLS OF MUSIC, NURSING, HEALTH EDUCATION PROGRAMS, DEPARTMENTS OF ELEMENTARY EDUCATION, MARKETING, JOURNALISM AND COLLEGE OF BUSINESS ARE AMONG THE BEST IN THE COUNTRY. BSU IS ACHIEVING EXCELLENCE IN SPORTS.

BALL STATE UNIVERSITY

STADIUM

ADMINISTRATION BUILDING

PRACTICAL ARTS BUILDING

LEWELLEN AQUATIC CENTER

Ball State University II

Kanwar Prakash Singh
© may 1989

BALL STATE UNIVERSITY *Muncie, Indiana*

Living with Hope

Hope, like faith, is essential for human survival, success, and happiness. Hope is a universal life-sustaining anchor that is recognized in all cultures and traditions. Hope anticipates the positive outcome of our concerns, endeavors, and prayers; it offers a sense of optimism about what the future may hold for our lives when we are in the midst of great challenges.

Faith is the spirit of hope. It is belief in the unseen and yet unanswered petitions and prayers. Being hopeful is an act of trust in something greater than our temporal comprehension and imagination. It is an instinctive feeling springing from deep within that often affirms cherished blessings. Hope gives us Light amidst darkness, and an inner positive echo amidst uncertainty. Hope manifests itself as an energy that drives and sustains us during our passages through life's turbulent times. Hope transcends doubt, defeat, despair, and disappointment.

Hope is the spirit and breath of life itself. Hope defines our humanity. From the beginning of time, life has been nurtured by real or imagined hopes from within or without, reassuring faith-inspired messages, beliefs, or promises from above or below. When we least expect, the much-sought relief, reward, surprising breakthrough, or cherished blessing arrives.

Legends abound in all cultures about hope inspiring people to make lasting contributions to human civilization. Remember the countless acts of sacrifice and daring to vanquish forces of darkness to restore hope. Imagine the giant leaps of mankind on the wings of hope.

Sacred Heart Church
University of Notre Dame

Samar P. Singh
april 1983

SACRED HEART CHURCH *Notre Dame, Indiana*

THE UNIVERSITY OF NOTRE DAME WAS FOUNDED IN 1842 BY A YOUNG PRIEST , FATHER EDWARD F. SORIN , OF THE FRENCH MISSIONARY ORDER OF THE CONGREGATION OF HOLY CROSS., OVER THE NEXT 155 YEARS , THE UNIVERSITY OF NOTRE DAME WAS TO GROW INTO ONE OF THE FINEST CATHOLIC INSTITUTIONS OF HIGHER EDUCATION IN THE UNITED STATES. NOTRE DAME IS A PRESTIGIOUS ASSET FOR INDIANA.

TODAY NOTRE DAME IS A LEADING SYMBOL OF CATHOLIC CULTURE AND HERITAGE IN AMERICA . YOUNG MEN AND WOMEN OF ALL FAITHS , DIVERSE CULTURES AND FROM MANY COUNTRIES ARE ATTRACTED TO THE UNIVERSITY FOR ITS SCHOLASTIC AND SPORTS TRADITION AND ACADEMIC LEADERSHIP. THE UNIVERSITY OFFERS UNDERGRADUATE AND POSTBACCALAUREATE PROGRAMS IN MANY FIELDS SERVED BY A 970-MEMBER TEACHING-RESEARCH FACULTY AND 282 PROFESSIONAL SPECIALISTS. REV. EDWARD A. MALLOY CSC IS NOTRE DAME'S 16TH PRESIDENT. NOTRE DAME'S 1250-ACRE CAMPUS , JUST NORTH OF THE CITY OF SOUTH BEND, IS MAJESTIC IN BEAUTY AND SPIRIT.

University of Notre Dame II

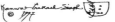

UNIVERSITY OF NOTRE DAME *Notre Dame, Indiana*

131

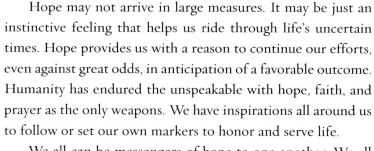

Hope may not arrive in large measures. It may be just an instinctive feeling that helps us ride through life's uncertain times. Hope provides us with a reason to continue our efforts, even against great odds, in anticipation of a favorable outcome. Humanity has endured the unspeakable with hope, faith, and prayer as the only weapons. We have inspirations all around us to follow or set our own markers to honor and serve life.

We all can be messengers of hope to one another. We all share hopes, dreams, and challenges. Extending hope to others is an act of faith and recognition of our common origin as God's children. All human efforts and dreams are threaded in hope. Hope offers us confidence to persevere. In hope, we recognize a friendly lifeline that helps us see beyond present challenges. To share and spread hope to others is living the true spirit of faith.

When hope is deeply enshrined in our soul, we can surmount unexpected events in our lives. We must never surrender to failure or defeat. We must always embrace hope for our individual and collective survival and prosperity. Where there is absence of hope, there is darkness, shadow, and death of spirit. Where there is hope, there is life, renewal, and triumph of spirit.

Everything we hope and pray for may not materialize. We know that millions upon this blessed earth daily witness the miracle and power of hope and God's unbounded Grace. Hope, like faith, beckons us to take heart, renew our strength, lift our spirit with a prayer and song, go forward with determination, prepare again to capture the blessing that we seek, and let God do the rest.

ST. MEINRAD *Indiana*

Saint Mary-of-the-Woods College
Saint Mary-of-the-Woods, Indiana
The Church of the Immaculate Conception - 1890

Lanwar P. Singh
November 1978

SAINT MARY-OF-THE-WOODS, INDIANA

The Chapel

Wabash College Crawfordsville, Indiana

1974

WABASH COLLEGE CHAPEL *Crawfordsville, Indiana*

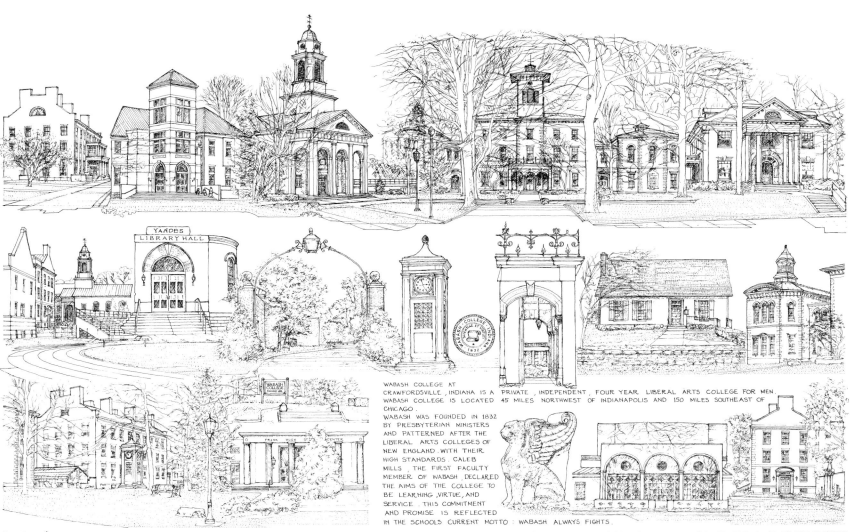

WABASH COLLEGE AT CRAWFORDSVILLE, INDIANA IS A PRIVATE, INDEPENDENT, FOUR YEAR LIBERAL ARTS COLLEGE FOR MEN. WABASH COLLEGE IS LOCATED 45 MILES NORTHWEST OF INDIANAPOLIS AND 150 MILES SOUTHEAST OF CHICAGO.

WABASH WAS FOUNDED IN 1832 BY PRESBYTERIAN MINISTERS AND PATTERNED AFTER THE LIBERAL ARTS COLLEGES OF NEW ENGLAND WITH THEIR HIGH STANDARDS. CALEB MILLS, THE FIRST FACULTY MEMBER OF WABASH, DECLARED THE AIMS OF THE COLLEGE TO BE LEARNING, VIRTUE, AND SERVICE. THIS COMMITMENT AND PROMISE IS REFLECTED IN THE SCHOOLS CURRENT MOTTO: WABASH ALWAYS FIGHTS.

THE SCHOOL'S 850 MALE STUDENTS COME FROM 34 STATES AND SEVERAL FOREIGN COUNTRIES. WABASH HAS COOPERATIVE STUDY ARRANGEMENTS WITH SEVERAL NATIONAL UNIVERSITIES FOR SOME OF THE 21 MAJORS OFFERED BY THE SCHOOL. IN ADDITION, WABASH OFFERS A WIDE RANGE OF SPORTS AND EXTRACURRICULAR ACTIVITIES. WABASH IS RANKED AMONG THE MOST PRESTIGIOUS LIBERAL ARTS COLLEGES IN THE NATION.

THE 55-ACRE WOODED CAMPUS NEAR DOWNTOWN CRAWFORDSVILLE, HOUSES 23 BUILDINGS, PREDOMINANTLY of GEORGIAN ARCHITECTURE, MANY OF THESE BUILDINGS DATE FROM THE EARLY 19TH CENTURY. THE COLLEGE CHAPEL IS THE CENTERPIECE OF THE CAMPUS ARCHITECTURAL AND HISTORIC LANDMARKS.

Wabash College II
Crawfordsville, Indiana

© 1998

WABASH COLLEGE *Crawfordsville, Indiana*

Mysteries and Miracles

In darkness and doubt,
We drift along paths of uncertainty,
Convinced it is as "ordained" for our lives.
We reach other shores,
 Find new visions and teachers,
Guiding others along new trails of promise.

Suddenly, new horizons float past our window,
New thresholds of promise come into sight,
New dreams fire our imagination.
We discover new visions, imagine new paths;
A new dance fills the "courtyard" of our spirit,
The "destined," with new promise and anticipation.

All Knowing Father,
Master of Mysteries and Miracles:
Leads and inspires us to seek higher, go farther.
All the while, all along the way
Changing, reshaping our journey, our Karma
Reaffirming: "I am the Lord God of all Creation."

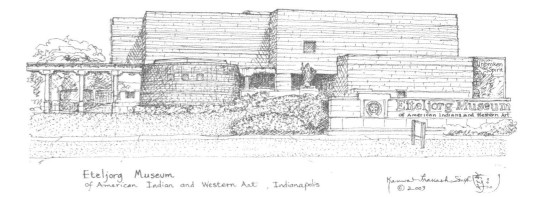

Eteljorg Museum
of American Indian and Western Art, Indianapolis
Kanwal Prakash Singh
© 2003

ETELJORG MUSEUM *Indianapolis, Indiana*

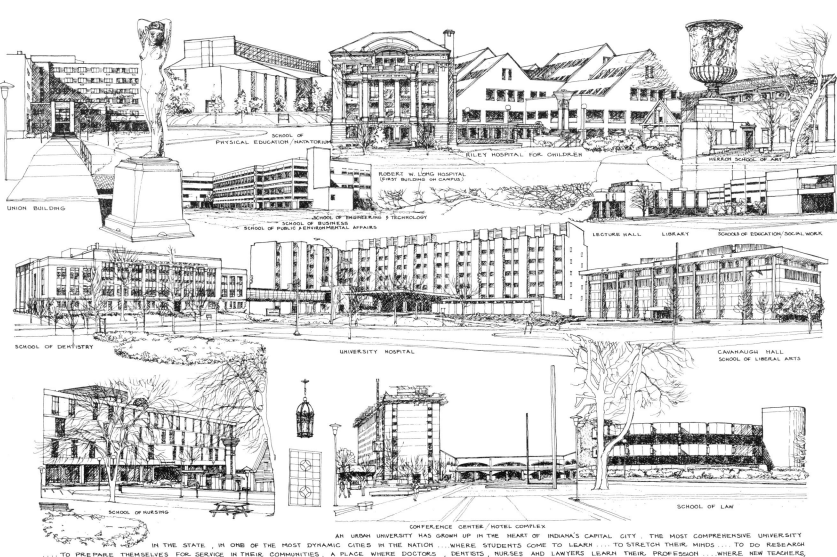

SCHOOL OF
PHYSICAL EDUCATION/NATATORIUM

RILEY HOSPITAL FOR CHILDREN

HERRON SCHOOL OF ART

UNION BUILDING

ROBERT W. LONG HOSPITAL
(FIRST BUILDING ON CAMPUS)

SCHOOL OF ENGINEERING & TECHNOLOGY
SCHOOL OF BUSINESS
SCHOOL OF PUBLIC & ENVIRONMENTAL AFFAIRS

LECTURE HALL   LIBRARY   SCHOOLS OF EDUCATION/SOCIAL WORK

SCHOOL OF DENTISTRY

UNIVERSITY HOSPITAL

CAVANAUGH HALL
SCHOOL OF LIBERAL ARTS

SCHOOL OF NURSING

CONFERENCE CENTER/HOTEL COMPLEX

SCHOOL OF LAW

AN URBAN UNIVERSITY HAS GROWN UP IN THE HEART OF INDIANA'S CAPITAL CITY. THE MOST COMPREHENSIVE UNIVERSITY IN THE STATE, IN ONE OF THE MOST DYNAMIC CITIES IN THE NATION ....WHERE STUDENTS COME TO LEARN .... TO STRETCH THEIR MINDS .... TO DO RESEARCH .... TO PREPARE THEMSELVES FOR SERVICE IN THEIR COMMUNITIES. A PLACE WHERE DOCTORS, DENTISTS, NURSES AND LAWYERS LEARN THEIR PROFESSION ....WHERE NEW TEACHERS, SOCIAL WORKERS, JOURNALISTS AND PUBLIC OFFICIALS HONE THEIR SKILLS ....WHERE SCIENTISTS AND ENGINEERS EXPLORE THE PROMISE OF TOMORROW. A PLACE FOR ARTISTS AND BUSINESSMEN, SCHOLARS IN THE LIBERAL ARTS, PHYSICAL EDUCATORS AND CONTINUING EDUCATION. ALL OF THIS IN A BEAUTIFUL URBAN SETTING, FEATURING SOME OF THE BEST ATHLETIC FACILITIES IN THE WORLD. AND ALL BECAUSE TWO GREAT UNIVERSITIES .... INDIANA AND PURDUE ....DECIDED TO MAKE IT SO.

Indiana University - Purdue University at Indianapolis

Kanwar Prakash Singh
april 1987

INDIANA UNIVERSITY-PURDUE UNIVERSITY *Indianapolis, Indiana*

Imagine a Journey of Discovery

I do not suffer from wanderlust. I am more comfortable in places and with people I know, but I enjoy traveling, seeing new places, old architecture, and learning about other cultures. I find links in spirit that resonate throughout the patterns and rhythms of human experience and civilization. Universal concepts about life further confirm the common thread that binds all humanity.

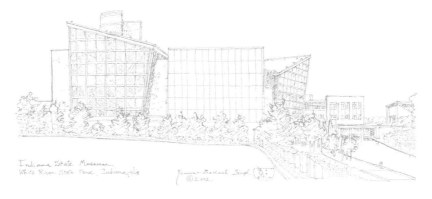

Indiana State Museum
White River State Park, Indianapolis

INDIANA STATE MUSEUM *Indianapolis, Indiana*

recreational, naval, and sight-seeing boats as we headed toward Chesapeake Bay and the Atlantic Ocean. Freighters were seen in the distance. Church steeples, spires, and the dome of the state capitol were soon a distant blur. It was fascinating to see the crew maneuver the 68-foot-tall yacht under the mighty four-mile-long bridge that connects Annapolis to the eastern shores of Maryland.

One recent summer, I visited historic Annapolis, Maryland. Located on the Severn River, with many attractions and well-preserved historic sites, Annapolis' waterfront also provides terrific sailing opportunities. Sailing on a yacht was a new experience for me. Our 75-foot craft *Imagine* was a vision of adventure and romance. I thought *Imagine* was a beautiful name for a sailboat.

Imagination is the foundation of creativity and a way to understand life and our place in the universe. Imagination inspires faith and belief in what we have not seen or experienced. Shortly after we left the dock, the sails went up. We passed many

I began to imagine all the bridges that connect communities and countries, making the earth a global village. I began to wonder what hopes and dreams traveled on these waters. What were the challenges and hardships faced by early settlers to build communities in the image of their native lands and shape the framework of a new nation? I marveled at those who dreamed, dared, sacrificed, and succeeded in a giant leap of faith and exploration.

Reflections of mankind were mirrored before me. I saw manifestations of God's glory all around. I imagined rivers, lakes, and

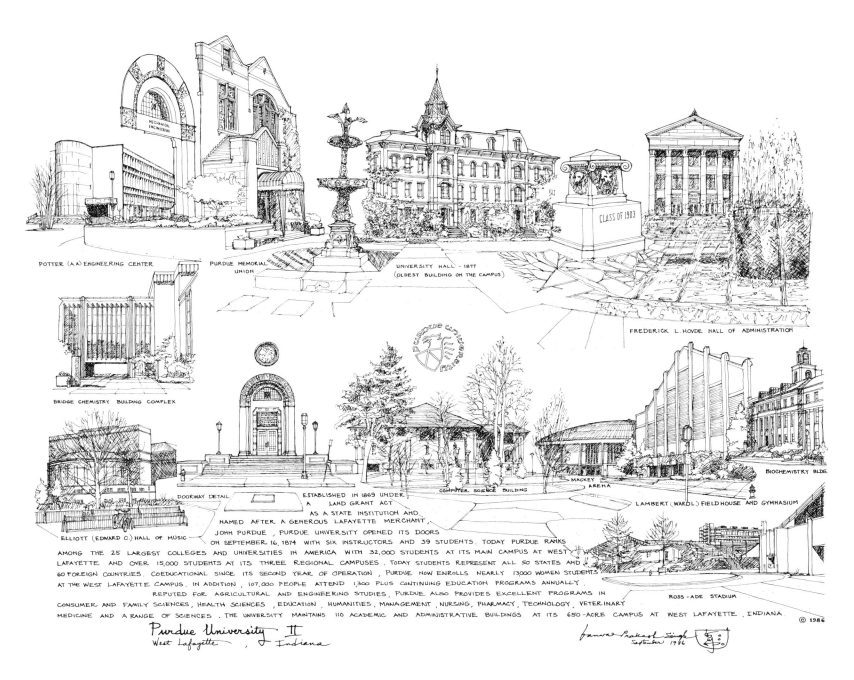

POTTER (A.A.) ENGINEERING CENTER

PURDUE MEMORIAL UNION

UNIVERSITY HALL - 1877
(OLDEST BUILDING ON THE CAMPUS)

CLASS OF 1903

FREDERICK L. HOVDE HALL OF ADMINISTRATION

BRIDGE CHEMISTRY BUILDING COMPLEX

DOORWAY DETAIL

COMPUTER SCIENCE BUILDING

MACKEY ARENA

BIOCHEMISTRY BLDG.

LAMBERT (WARD L.) FIELD HOUSE AND GYMNASIUM

ELLIOTT (EDWARD C.) HALL OF MUSIC

ROSS-ADE STADIUM

ESTABLISHED IN 1869 UNDER A LAND GRANT ACT AS A STATE INSTITUTION AND NAMED AFTER A GENEROUS LAFAYETTE MERCHANT, JOHN PURDUE, PURDUE UNIVERSITY OPENED ITS DOORS ON SEPTEMBER 16, 1874 WITH SIX INSTRUCTORS AND 39 STUDENTS. TODAY PURDUE RANKS AMONG THE 25 LARGEST COLLEGES AND UNIVERSITIES IN AMERICA WITH 32,000 STUDENTS AT ITS MAIN CAMPUS AT WEST LAFAYETTE AND OVER 15,000 STUDENTS AT ITS THREE REGIONAL CAMPUSES. TODAY STUDENTS REPRESENT ALL 50 STATES AND 60 FOREIGN COUNTRIES. COEDUCATIONAL SINCE ITS SECOND YEAR OF OPERATION, PURDUE NOW ENROLLS NEARLY 13,000 WOMEN STUDENTS AT THE WEST LAFAYETTE CAMPUS. IN ADDITION, 107,000 PEOPLE ATTEND 1,300 PLUS CONTINUING EDUCATION PROGRAMS ANNUALLY.
REPUTED FOR AGRICULTURAL AND ENGINEERING STUDIES, PURDUE ALSO PROVIDES EXCELLENT PROGRAMS IN CONSUMER AND FAMILY SCIENCES, HEALTH SCIENCES, EDUCATION, HUMANITIES, MANAGEMENT, NURSING, PHARMACY, TECHNOLOGY, VETERINARY MEDICINE AND A RANGE OF SCIENCES. THE UNIVERSITY MAINTAINS 110 ACADEMIC AND ADMINISTRATIVE BUILDINGS AT ITS 650-ACRE CAMPUS AT WEST LAFAYETTE, INDIANA.

© 1986

Purdue University II
West Lafayette, Indiana

Banwar Prakash Singh
September 1986

PURDUE UNIVERSITY *Lafayette, Indiana*

HERMAN MOENCH HALL

THE CAIRN

ROSE-HULMAN INSTITUTE OF TECHNOLOGY

HULMAN MEMORIAL UNION

DEMING HALL

ROSE HULMAN INSTITUTE OF TECHNOLOGY IS ONE OF THE SELECT FEW INDEPENDENT COLLEGES OF ENGINEERING AND SCIENCE IN THE UNITED STATES. IT WAS FOUNDED IN 1874 BY CHAUNCEY ROSE, A PIONEER INDUSTRIALIST AND ENTREPRENEUR.
ON JANUARY 6, 1971, THE NAME OF THE COLLEGE WAS CHANGED FROM ROSE POLYTECHNIC INSTITUTE TO ROSE HULMAN INSTITUTE OF TECHNOLOGY IN RECOGNITION OF NEARLY A CENTURY OF SUPPORT FROM HULMAN FAMILY OF TERRE HAUTE, INDIANA.
THE CURRENT ENROLLMENT OF 1200 IS DRAWN FROM 45 STATES. THE INSTITUTE OFFERS BACHELOR OF SCIENCE DEGREES IN CHEMISTRY, COMPUTER SCIENCE, MATHEMATICS, MATHEMATICAL ECONOMICS, PHYSICS, CIVIL, ELECTRICAL AND MECHANICAL ENGINEERING AND A LIMITED MASTER'S PROGRAM IN SOME OF THESE AREAS OF STUDY. SEVENTY PERCENT OF THE STUDENTS ARE INVOLVED IN INTRAMURAL ACTIVITIES WHICH ARE AN INTEGRAL PART OF THE EDUCATIONAL PHILOSOPHY AT ROSE HULMAN.

Rose Hulman Institute of Technology
Terre Haute, Indiana

Kanwal P. Singh
May 1981

oceanfronts providing spectacular settings for cities and civilizations, linking people and settlements, countries and continents. I saw life as a river and water as a symbol of the coexistence and interdependence between man and nature.

Our communion with water, folklore of the seas, and location of pilgrimage sites emerge from our universal fascination with water. Baptismal ceremonies, ritual baths, purification rites, and immersion of cremation ashes in sacred rivers affirm the importance of water in faith traditions.

I imagined monarchs sending armies across uncharted seas to expand their kingdoms, influence, and wealth. Others set out to discover unexplored regions, expand trade routes, visit learning and spiritual centers, establish new religions, or engage in high adventure. Faith, fortune, passion, and imagination guided the journey and destiny of man. The lives of dreamers and pioneers remind us "to strive" for and discover new frontiers, build new monuments, and imagine the unimagined.

I was still indulging in my voyage of reflection when suddenly the church steeples and the state capitol dome appeared glistening in the afternoon sun. *Imagine* stirred some new emotions deep within me. Like those before us, each of us could be a bridge to new discoveries and possibilities. Imagine that!

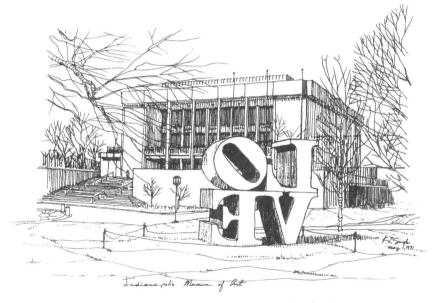

INDIANAPOLIS MUSEUM OF ART *Indianapolis, Indiana*

The CHILDREN'S MUSEUM OF INDIANAPOLIS

June 15, 1996

Peter V. Sterling
President

Euna Pittman
Chairman of the Board

Where children grow up......
and adults don't have to!

The Children's Museum of Indianapolis

Kanwal Prakash Singh
© June 1996

WELL HOUSE

THE BROWN MEMORIAL CHAPEL

PARKER AUDITORIUM

THE J. GRAHAM BROWN CAMPUS CENTER

SCIENCE HALL

DONNER HALL

PRESIDENT'S HOME

HENDRICKS HALL

FOUNDED JANUARY 1, 1827, HANOVER IS DISTINGUISHED AS THE OLDEST
PRIVATE COLLEGE FOUR YEAR LIBERAL ARTS COLLEGE IN INDIANA. AS THE ONLY PRESBYTERIAN
COLLEGE IN INDIANA, HANOVER WAS FOUNDED BY REVEREND JOHN FINLEY CROWE D.D. ACTING UNDER THE APPOINT-
MENT BY MADISON PRESBYTERY, SYNOD OF KENTUCKY PRESBYTERIAN CHURCH.
LOCATED IN THE SOUTHEASTERN CORNER OF INDIANA, HANOVER COLLEGE IS NEARLY IN THE CENTER OF A TRIANGLE FORMED BY
CINCINNATI, LOUISVILLE, INDIANAPOLIS. ALTHOUGH THERE ARE STRONG CULTURAL AND ECONOMIC TIES BETWEEN
THE COLLEGE AND THESE COMMUNITIES, IN A REAL SENSE, THE COLLEGE IS A CULTURAL AND INTELLECTUAL CENTER IN ITSELF.
HANOVER IS A COMPLETE ACADEMIC COMMUNITY OVERLOOKING AN INSPIRING PANORAMA OF THE MIGHTY OHIO RIVER AND ITS VALLEY. TODAY IT IS A MODERN COLLEGE LOCATED ON 555 ACRES WITH ITS
BEAUTIFUL GEORGIAN ARCHITECTURE BUILDINGS CONTAINING THE MOST UP TO DATE EDUCATIONAL FACILITIES FOR ITS 1000 STUDENTS FROM 34 STATES AND 12 FOREIGN COUNTRIES PURSUING 26 DISCIPLINES.

NOVEMBER 1979

HANOVER COLLEGE *Hanover, Indiana*

DEPAUW UNIVERSITY IS LOCATED ABOUT 45 MILES WEST ... OF INDIANAPOLIS. FOUNDED IN 1837 BY THE UNITED METHODIST CHURCH, IT IS TODAY AN UNDERGRADUATE, LIBERAL ARTS CO-EDUCATION COLLEGE WITH AN ENROLLMENT ... OF 2300 STUDENTS FROM 44 STATES AND 15 FOREIGN COUNTRIES. DEPAUW HAS ESTABLISHED ITSELF AS A LEADER ... AMONG SMALL COLLEGES " WITH A TRADITION OF UNCOMMON SUCCESS OF ITS GRADUATES AS FUTURE BUSINESS LEADERS". U.S. NEWS & WORLD REPORT RANKS DEPAUW AS ONE OF AMERICA'S TOP 50 LIBERAL ARTS AND SCIENCE COLLEGES. DEPAUW PRIDES ITSELF IN "OFFERING EXCELLENT ACADEMIC ENVIRONMENT AND GLOBAL OUTREACH" WITH AN "UNPARALLELED INTERNSHIP PROGRAM AT CORPORATE, SCIENTIFIC AND NON-PROFIT SITES ACROSS THE USA AND THROUGHOUT THE WORLD."

THE BEAUTIFUL DEPAUW CAMPUS INCLUDES RESTORED HISTORIC BUILDINGS ALONG SIDE THE STATE-OF-THE ARTS FACILITIES ON ITS 175-ACRE CAMPUS AT GREENCASTLE, INDIANA. THE EAST COLLEGE, THE ARCHITECTURAL CENTERPIECE IS ON THE NATIONAL REGISTER OF HISTORIC PLACES.

DePauw University II

Kanwar Avtesh Singh
© 1777

EAST COLLEGE - "HISTORIC CENTERPIECE" 1884
DEPAUW UNIVERSITY - FOUNDED IN 1837 - GREENCASTLE, INDIANA, U.S.A.

Kanwar Prakash Singh 1996

Mandate to Nurture the Living

ELI LILLY AND COMPANY is a global research-based pharmaceutical corporation. The Company was founded by Colonel Eli Lilly, a veteran of the U.S. Civil War, in May 1876. Eli Lilly and Company today employs 31,000 people worldwide and markets its products in 179 countries.

Eli Lilly and Company
Indianapolis, Indiana, U.S.A.

ELI LILLY AND COMPANY *Indianapolis, Indiana*

Give new gifts, reach for new heavens. These lines from the song of the Buddhist monks tempt our imagination to a higher spiritual horizon, inviting us to share and serve others with our gifts and opportunities. The Sikh faith advocates the importance of doing Seva (selfless service and sharing with faith and humility). For a Sikh, Seva is a spiritual and moral responsibility to enhance life and nurture the living.

Seva has been a force for good in society. Seva is a lifeline of hope, our faith at work, a testament of spiritual lessons learned. Through Seva, we make a difference for those among us who are challenged by circumstances, events, disasters, or destiny. Seva is an act of understanding and compassion toward all living beings.

Everyone can be God's helping hand. We are His workforce, His frontline for caring and serving. Seva blesses the one who serves and the recipient. Christ assures us of a personal relationship with the Lord when we serve: "Do unto the least among you, and you do unto Me."

Sikh scriptures affirm the message "God is love; to love God is to love all His creation; every act of kindness is an offering to Him." Seva opens our spiritual window and lets God's Light in, "Make thy living by honest labors and share thy blessings with the needy, Nanak [founder of Sikhism] sayeth, such souls have discovered the true way to God."

The sacred key to such a blessing is "Seva and 'Simran' (meditation and remembrance of His Name)." Seva and Simran, "purify the mind and spirit of all ailments that separate us from God." The Sikh scriptures advocate serving with "tuhn" (labors/talents),

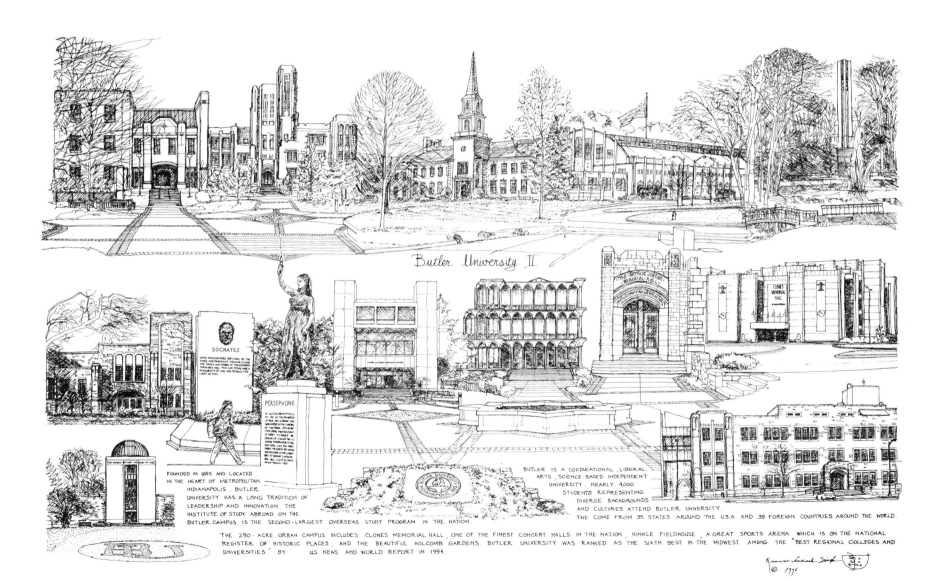

Butler University II

SOCRATES

PERSEPHONE

FOUNDED IN 1855 AND LOCATED IN THE HEART OF METROPOLITAN INDIANAPOLIS, BUTLER UNIVERSITY HAS A LONG TRADITION OF LEADERSHIP AND INNOVATION. THE INSTITUTE OF STUDY ABROAD ON THE BUTLER CAMPUS IS THE SECOND-LARGEST OVERSEAS STUDY PROGRAM IN THE NATION.

BUTLER IS A COEDUCATIONAL, LIBERAL ARTS, SCIENCE-BASED INDEPENDENT UNIVERSITY. NEARLY 4,000 STUDENTS REPRESENTING DIVERSE BACKGROUNDS AND CULTURES ATTEND BUTLER UNIVERSITY. THE COME FROM 35 STATES AROUND THE U.S.A. AND 39 FOREIGN COUNTRIES AROUND THE WORLD.

THE 290-ACRE URBAN CAMPUS INCLUDES CLOWES MEMORIAL HALL, ONE OF THE FINEST CONCERT HALLS IN THE NATION, HINKLE FIELDHOUSE, A GREAT SPORTS ARENA WHICH IS ON THE NATIONAL REGISTER OF HISTORIC PLACES, AND THE BEAUTIFUL HOLCOMB GARDENS. BUTLER UNIVERSITY WAS RANKED AS THE SIXTH BEST IN THE MIDWEST AMONG THE "BEST REGIONAL COLLEGES AND UNIVERSITIES" BY U.S. NEWS AND WORLD REPORT IN 1994.

BUTLER UNIVERSITY *Indianapolis, Indiana*

"muhn" (mind/spirit), and "dhun" (resources)—all gifts that God has entrusted to us. A life without Seva and Simran is "an opportunity lost."

His Holiness Dalai Lama reminds us about compassion. Mother Teresa and Bhagat Puran Singh (founder of a home for the disabled in Amritsar, India) exemplify service, sacrifice, and suffering to bring hope and dignity to others. Such divinely inspired souls offer inspiration to many. The network of support organizations and vital services performed by dedicated volunteers offer a second chance at life to many, survival to others. I shall never forget total strangers offering help and comfort to devastated, victims of the horrors of the Partition of India in 1947. That is God's love at work.

One must ask, "what can I do" for the well-being of my community and for the cause of humanity? Community food banks, soup kitchens, homeless shelters, global relief efforts, and thousands of critical programs offer opportunities to serve.

Seva dismantles barriers of separateness and fosters a sense of kinship. True seva transcends all ethnic, religious, cultural, territorial, and material considerations. Movement of people and cultures across traditional frontiers demands that we explore emerging areas of service in our communities. Suffering and adversity do not discriminate; they trespass all boundaries. Seva is always all-embracing.

The responsibility to serve is an important measure of our humanity. Seva as an expression and extension of our faith may bring us in touch with our deeper Self, maybe even an encounter with the sacred or divine. Then again, it might not. We must, in faithful affirmation, honor the call of the Buddhist monks and other sacred voices. Seva is its own reward. We should remember that we would need worthy offerings for our journey "Home."

SHORTRIDGE HIGH SCHOOL *Indianapolis, Indiana*

BREBEUF JESUIT PREPARATORY SCHOOL

BREBEUF JESUIT PREPARATORY SCHOOL WAS FOUNDED IN 1961 BY THE SOCIETY OF JESUS. THE SCHOOL BUILDING WAS BUILT ON A SIXTY-ACRE LOT, ONCE IN THE RURAL FARMLAND, NOW AT THE HUB OF A COMMERCIAL AND RESIDENTIAL AREA ON THE NORTHWEST SIDE OF INDIANAPOLIS, INDIANA.

BREBEUF JESUIT SERVES ABOUT 700 STUDENTS ANNUALLY IN GRADES 9-12. THE STUDENT BODY REPRESENTS MANY ETHNIC, CULTURAL AND RELIGIOUS BACKGROUNDS. THE SCHOOL IS DEDICATED TO THE PRINCIPLES AND IDEALS OF ST. IGNATIUS LOYOLA, FOUNDER OF THE SOCIETY OF JESUS. IT IS RECOGNIZED FOR ITS STUDENTS OF EXCEPTIONAL ABILITY, ADULT LEADERS WHO DEMONSTRATE UNCOMMON CARING, AND ADHERENCE TO THE 450-YEAR-OLD TRADITION OF JESUIT EDUCATIONAL EXCELLENCE.

PROMOTING "FAITH AND JUSTICE", INSPIRING "MEN AND WOMEN FOR OTHERS", AND WORKING TO "CORRECT INJUSTICE" ARE ALL CENTRAL ELEMENTS OF A CURRICULUM THAT COMBINES RIGOROUS ACADEMIC STUDY WITH A STRONG COMMITMENT TO FAITH, DIVERSITY AND COMMUNITY SERVICE.

DINING HALL

ADMINISTRATION BLDG

MEMORIAL CHAPEL

RIDING HALL

MEMORIAL LIBRARY

CLASS OF 1976

EUGENE C. EPPLEY AUDITORIUM

GIGNILLIAT MEMORIAL BLDG.

EPPLEY HALL OF SCIENCE

THE SHACK

CLASS 1936

HERE, IN 1894, WITH THIS BOULDER AS HIS WORKBENCH AND NATURE'S OWN OUT-OF-DOORS FOR HIS SHOP HENRY HARRISON CULVER FASHIONED OUT OF THE MISTS OF HIS BOYHOOD DREAM THE FRAMEWORK OF A SCHOOL--A SCHOOL WHERE THE YOUTH OF ONCOMING YEARS SHOULD BE FORGED INTO MEN FIT FOR THE CITIZENSHIP OF THE MORROW.

CULVER MILITARY ACADEMY, FOUNDED IN 1894 BY ST. LOUIS MANUFACTURER - HENRY HARRISON CULVER, IS RECOGNIZED TODAY AS ONE OF THE TRULY OUTSTANDING COLLEGE PREPATORY BOARDING SCHOOL IN THE NATION. THE CAMPUS OF CULVER, WITH ITS 37 MAJOR BUILDINGS OCCUPIES 1500 ACRES OF BEAUTIFUL ROLLING HILLS AND WOODLANDS, A MAJOR PORTION OF WHICH BORDERS LAKE MAXINKUCKEE. IN 1894, THE ACADEMY OPENED WITH 45 CADETS. IN RECENT YEARS, THE COMBINED ENROLLMENT OF CULVER MILITARY ACADEMY AND CULVER GIRLS ACADEMY (FOUNDED IN 1971) HAS AVERAGED ABOUT 750 _ REPRESENTING STUDENTS FROM 40 STATES AND 20 FOREIGN COUNTRIES. CULVER OFFERS ACADEMIC AND EXTRA CURRICULAR OPPORTUNITIES IN MANY AREAS INCLUDING NAVAL, HORSEMANSHIP AND AVIATION. CULVER IS THE HOME OF THE WORLD FAMOUS BLACK HORSE TROOP AND IS THE LARGEST EQUISTRIAN SCHOOL IN U.S. CULVER SEEKS EXCELLENCE IN ALL IT DOES.

Culver Military Academy, Culver, Indiana

Sawwa P. Singh
September 1983

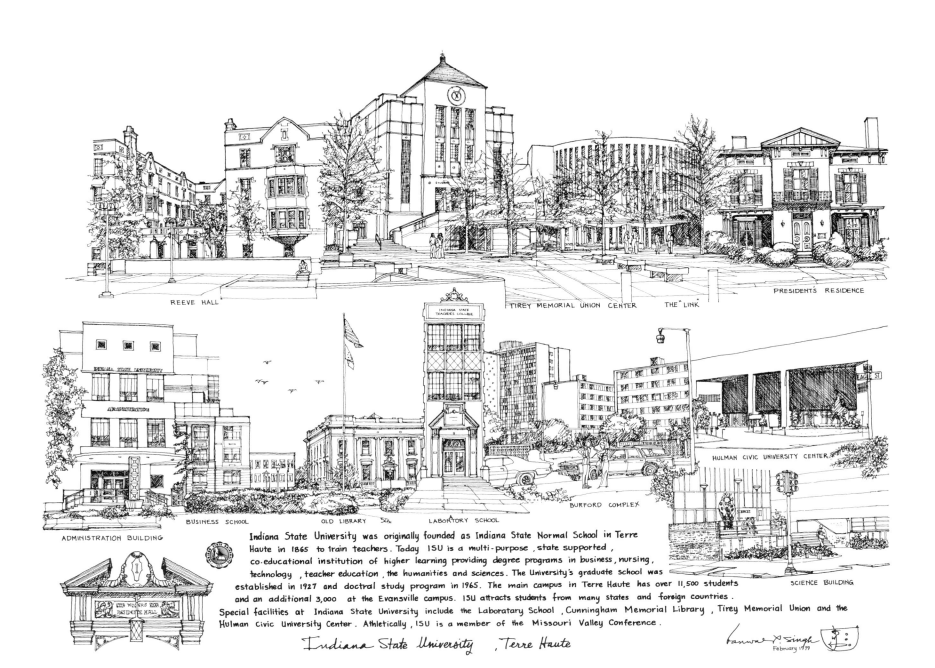

REEVE HALL

TIREY MEMORIAL UNION CENTER

THE "LINK"

PRESIDENTS RESIDENCE

ADMINISTRATION BUILDING

BUSINESS SCHOOL

OLD LIBRARY

LABORTORY SCHOOL

BURFORD COMPLEX

HULMAN CIVIC UNIVERSITY CENTER

SCIENCE BUILDING

Indiana State University was originally founded as Indiana State Normal School in Terre Haute in 1865 to train teachers. Today ISU is a multi-purpose, state supported, co-educational institution of higher learning providing degree programs in business, nursing, technology, teacher education, the humanities and sciences. The University's graduate school was established in 1927 and doctral study program in 1965. The main campus in Terre Haute has over 11,500 students and an additional 3,000 at the Evansville campus. ISU attracts students from many states and foreign countries. Special facilities at Indiana State University include the Laboratary School, Cunningham Memorial Library, Tirey Memorial Union and the Hulman Civic University Center. Athletically, ISU is a member of the Missouri Valley Conference.

Indiana State University, Terre Haute

February 1979

INDIANA CENTRAL UNIVERSITY WAS ORGANIZED ABOUT THE TURN OF THE CENTURY BY THE CHURCH OF THE UNITED BRETHREN IN CHRIST, A PREDECESSOR OF THE UNITED METHODIST CHURCH. TODAY ITS CAMPUS ON THE SOUTH SIDE OF INDIANAPOLIS, PROVIDES QUALITY "EDUCATION FOR SERVICE" FOR 7500 FULL-TIME/PART-TIME/CONTINUING EDUCATION STUDENTS FROM MANY STATES AND FOREIGN COUNTRIES THROUGH ITS MANY EDUCATIONAL, SPORTS, CULTURAL AND RELATED PROGRAMS.

Indiana Central University
Indianapolis, Indiana

Kanwar P. Singh
February 1981

INDIANA CENTRAL UNIVERSITY *Indianapolis, Indiana*

HIGHER EDUCATION COMMITTED TO THE DIGNITY OF THE INDIVIDUAL, RESPONSIBLE STEWARDSHIP, RECONCILIATION, PEACE AND JUSTICE." AT MARIAN CONSIDERABLE PRIDE IS TAKEN IN HELPING STUDENTS GROW BY DEVELOPING THEIR MULTIDIMENSIONAL THINKING." — DR. DANIEL A. FELICETTI, PRESIDENT.

FOUNDED AND SPONSORED BY THE SISTERS OF ST. FRANCIS OLDENBURG, INDIANA. SINCE 1851

MOVED TO INDIANAPOLIS OFFERING ACADEMICS IN LIBERAL ARTS TRADITION. SINCE 1937

O Divine Master,
Grant that I may not so much
seek to be consoled as to console;
To be understood as to understand;
To be loved as to love.
For it is in giving
that we receive.....

Marian College II
Indianapolis, Indiana, USA

MARIAN COLLEGE *Indianapolis, Indiana*

THE TRIANGULAR WALKER BUILDING AND THEATRE IS
A SIGNIFICANT LANDMARK LOCATED ON INDIANA AVENUE.
DESIGNED IN 1927 BY ARCHITECTS RUBUSH AND HUNTER,
THE STRUCTURE IS NAMED AFTER MADAME C.J. WALKER,
THE NATION'S FIRST BLACK FEMALE MILLIONAIRE.
WITH ITS AFRO-EGYPTIAN TERRA COTTA MOTIFS,
THE THEATRE HAS SERVED AS AN ENTERTAINMENT
MECCA TO AREA RESIDENTS, PROVIDING POSITIVE
SYMBOLS OF BLACK COMMUNITY PRIDE AND INDIVIDUAL
ACHIEVEMENT.

The Walker Theatre

THE WALKER BUILDING IS LISTED ON THE
STATE AND NATIONAL REGISTER OF HISTORIC PLACES.

RECENT RESTORATION OF THE BUILDING BY THE MADAME C.J.
WALKER URBAN LIFE CENTER, INC., AND OTHER REVITALI-
ZATION EFFORTS THROUGHOUT THE AREA ARE BRINGING
NEW VITALITY TO "THE AVENUE" AND THE CITY OF
INDIANAPOLIS.

ORIGINAL ARTWORK COMMISSIONED BY AMERICAN
CABLEVISION OF INDIANAPOLIS FOR THE HBO PREMIERE
SCREENING OF "THE JOSEPHINE BAKER STORY" AT THE
WALKER THEATRE IN INDIANAPOLIS, IND. FEBRUARY 21, 1991.

Kanwal Prakash Singh
© February 1991

THE WALKER THEATRE *Indianapolis, Indiana*

Diversity Can Enrich
Our Lives and Culture

The cultural texture of America is becoming more colorful as people flock to our shores from the remotest corners of the earth. This transformation must be viewed as a blessing, bringing new energy, talents, and creativity for our future. First, we must understand the true importance of this cultural challenge.

Our culture, ethnicity, and faith are deeply enshrined in our soul. They give each of us our identity. For many, culture and tradition border on the sacred, a vital life-force and inheritance that may define their very being. Diversity offers America new vitality, strength, and global perspective. Therefore, our discussions should focus on how best to preserve, enhance, nurture, and celebrate our growing multicultural spirit in America; encourage "winds of culture" to flow through our communities.

There is enough evidence to support the view that we are all better human beings when along with the abundant temporal comforts and blessings, we are also assured a full measure of basic cultural and spiritual rights and respect. For new immigrants, it is all the more essential for adaptation to their new

Old Main - Administration Building
Franklin College, Indiana

FRANKLIN COLLEGE *Franklin, Indiana*

environment. We also must make sure that "diversity" does not mean infringing or threatening other cultures.

As an immigrant American living in Indiana since 1967 and a follower of the Sikh faith tradition, I am well aware of the challenges and the promise of cultural diversity in American communities. I believe that new ideas, ideals, traditions and cultures can only enrich the American experience and character. Expanded understanding of the people who inhabit this planet and share a common destiny can bridge many divides that separate us today.

Diversity in itself is no threat to American sovereignty, way of life, and founding principles. We must adopt and extend a more enlightened understanding toward all new citizens and transcending cultures in our midst. No one needs to "leave" his or her true "spirit" behind to be part of this great nation and to be a good American.

PERFORMING ARTS CENTER

MARTIN UNIVERSITY *Indianapolis, Indiana*

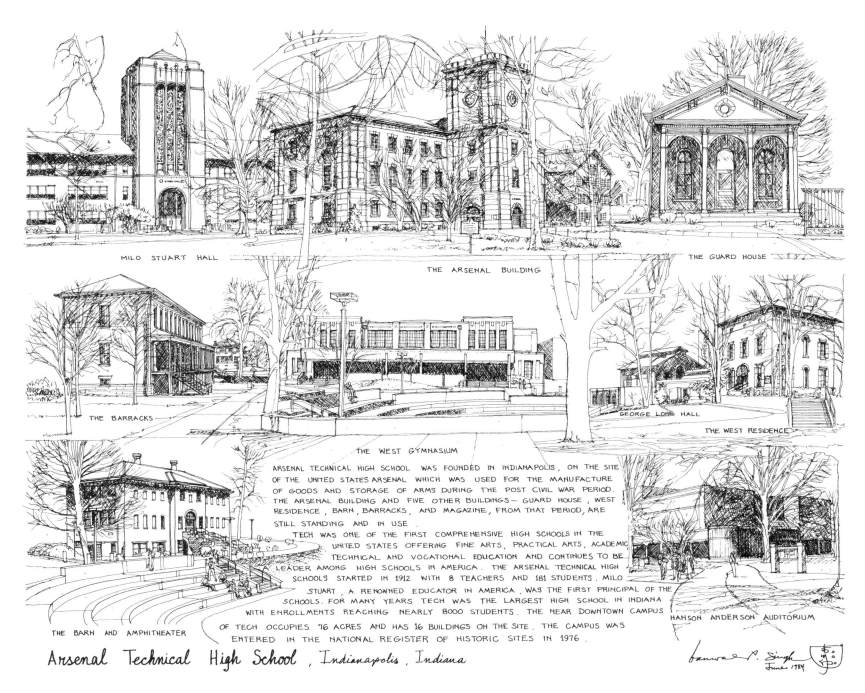

MILO STUART HALL

THE ARSENAL BUILDING

THE GUARD HOUSE

THE BARRACKS

THE WEST GYMNASIUM

GEORGE LONG HALL

THE WEST RESIDENCE

THE BARN AND AMPHITHEATER

ARSENAL TECHNICAL HIGH SCHOOL WAS FOUNDED IN INDIANAPOLIS, ON THE SITE OF THE UNITED STATES ARSENAL WHICH WAS USED FOR THE MANUFACTURE OF GOODS AND STORAGE OF ARMS DURING THE POST CIVIL WAR PERIOD. THE ARSENAL BUILDING AND FIVE OTHER BUILDINGS— GUARD HOUSE, WEST RESIDENCE, BARN, BARRACKS, AND MAGAZINE, FROM THAT PERIOD, ARE STILL STANDING AND IN USE.
TECH WAS ONE OF THE FIRST COMPREHENSIVE HIGH SCHOOLS IN THE UNITED STATES OFFERING FINE ARTS, PRACTICAL ARTS, ACADEMIC TECHNICAL AND VOCATIONAL EDUCATION AND CONTINUES TO BE LEADER AMONG HIGH SCHOOLS IN AMERICA. THE ARSENAL TECHNICAL HIGH SCHOOLS STARTED IN 1912 WITH 8 TEACHERS AND 181 STUDENTS. MILO STUART, A RENOWNED EDUCATOR IN AMERICA, WAS THE FIRST PRINCIPAL OF THE SCHOOLS. FOR MANY YEARS TECH WAS THE LARGEST HIGH SCHOOL IN INDIANA WITH ENROLLMENTS REACHING NEARLY 8000 STUDENTS. THE NEAR DOWNTOWN CAMPUS OF TECH OCCUPIES 76 ACRES AND HAS 16 BUILDINGS ON THE SITE. THE CAMPUS WAS ENTERED IN THE NATIONAL REGISTER OF HISTORIC SITES IN 1976.

HANSON ANDERSON AUDITORIUM

Arsenal Technical High School, Indianapolis, Indiana

Sanwal P. Singh
June 1984

ARSENAL TECHNICAL HIGH SCHOOL *Indianapolis, Indiana*

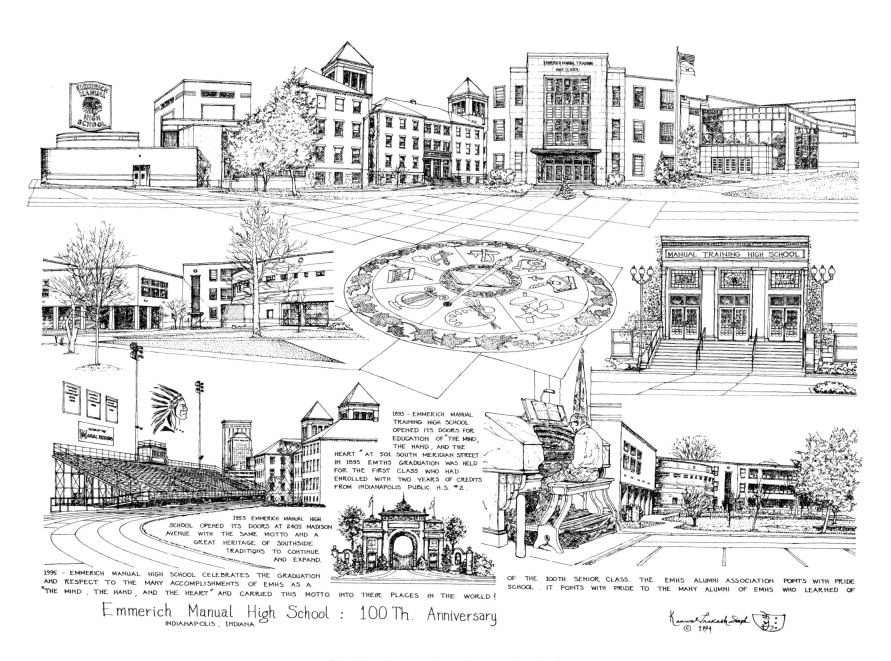

1893 - EMMERICH MANUAL TRAINING HIGH SCHOOL OPENED ITS DOORS FOR EDUCATION OF "THE MIND, THE HAND, AND THE HEART" AT 501 SOUTH MERIDIAN STREET. IN 1895 EMTHS GRADUATION WAS HELD FOR THE FIRST CLASS WHO HAD ENROLLED WITH TWO YEARS OF CREDITS FROM INDIANAPOLIS PUBLIC H.S. #2.

1953 EMMERICH MANUAL HIGH SCHOOL OPENED ITS DOORS AT 2405 MADISON AVENUE WITH THE SAME MOTTO AND A GREAT HERITAGE OF SOUTHSIDE TRADITIONS TO CONTINUE AND EXPAND.

1995 - EMMERICH MANUAL HIGH SCHOOL CELEBRATES THE GRADUATION AND RESPECT TO THE MANY ACCOMPLISHMENTS OF EMHS AS A "THE MIND, THE HAND, AND THE HEART" AND CARRIED THIS MOTTO INTO THEIR PLACES IN THE WORLD!

OF THE 100TH. SENIOR CLASS. THE EMHS ALUMNI ASSOCIATION POINTS WITH PRIDE SCHOOL. IT POINTS WITH PRIDE TO THE MANY ALUMNI OF EMHS WHO LEARNED OF

Emmerich Manual High School : 100Th. Anniversary
INDIANAPOLIS, INDIANA

Kanwal Prakash Singh
© 1994

EMMERICH MANUAL HIGH SCHOOL *Indianapolis, Indiana*

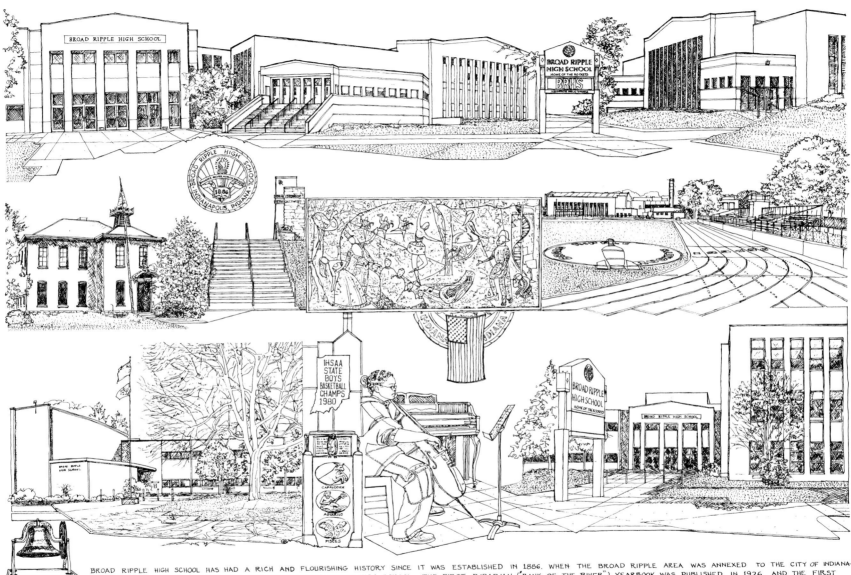

BROAD RIPPLE HIGH SCHOOL HAS HAD A RICH AND FLOURISHING HISTORY SINCE IT WAS ESTABLISHED IN 1886. WHEN THE BROAD RIPPLE AREA WAS ANNEXED TO THE CITY OF INDIANA-POLIS IN 1923, BRHS BECAME THE 4TH INDIANAPOLIS PUBLIC HIGH SCHOOL. THE FIRST *RIPARIAN* ("BANK OF THE RIVER") YEARBOOK WAS PUBLISHED IN 1926, AND THE FIRST *RIPARIAN* NEWSPAPER IN 1929. THE SCHOOL'S MOTTO ....BROADER RICHER HUMAN SERVICE .... WAS CREATED BY PRINCIPAL K.V. AMMERMAN IN 1935. THE STAFF AND ADMINISTRATORS HAVE ALWAYS STRESSED ACADEMIC EXCELLENCE. MANY RIPPLE ROCKETS ATHLETIC TEAMS HAVE EXCELLED OVER THE YEARS. BROAD RIPPLE BECAME THE CENTER FOR HUMANITIES IN 1979, AND THE CENTER FOR PERFORMING ARTS IN 1981. ENROLLMENT FOR THE 2001-2002 ACADEMIC SCHOOL YEAR WAS 1,591.

TODAY, BROAD RIPPLE HIGH SCHOOL IS LOCATED IN THE HEART OF THE CITY IN THE VILLAGE OF BROAD RIPPLE, AND OFFERS ITS STUDENTS THE OPPORTUNITY TO DEVELOP THE LIFE-SHAPING PRINCIPLES OF FREEDOM, RESPECT, HONOR, AND INTEGRITY.

Broad Ripple High School, Indianapolis, Indiana

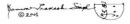

©2001

Ideas That Inspire

Our circumstances and experiences fashion our ideas. We float our ideas and dreams across the river of life in search of our destiny. Only some of the ideas, hopes, and endeavors survive the tumble and turbulence of the journey. If we are fortunate, we may leave behind a few worthy gifts that capture the essence of our lives and reflect our unique spirit.

Today, all around us, we witness the convergence of the many wonderful ideas of daring dreamers. Their unimaginable gifts and unmatched spirit enrich and define our civilization. Their wisdom and sacrifices provide light to guide our ship safely through the rough waters and dark moments. Such souls offer us hope, faith, and inspiration. They show us the way and lead us forward on our journey.

Great souls change the course of our lives. They invite us to study the new sheets of music with an

CHATEAU CHAUMONT *Loire Valley, France*

unfamiliar melody. Such enlightened individuals inspire us to embark on a voyage to unknown and unexplored destinations.

New visions and ideas take birth. We strive to expand life's rhythms to a new measure, unravel a few mysteries, maybe paint a fresh vision on the old canvas of life or write a new epic of adventure. Great souls bear witness to life and spirit in the highest. They inspire each of us to imitate and honor life with new gifts and reach for new heavens.

When that happens, we are no longer adrift; we awaken to capture the moment, putting past failures and fears behind. Our spirit comes to life, and life no longer wanders in the shadows of uncertainty. With a leap of faith, we rush toward the light knowing that the windows in life may be open for a brief time. We understand that great ideas cannot wait. One must give them shape.

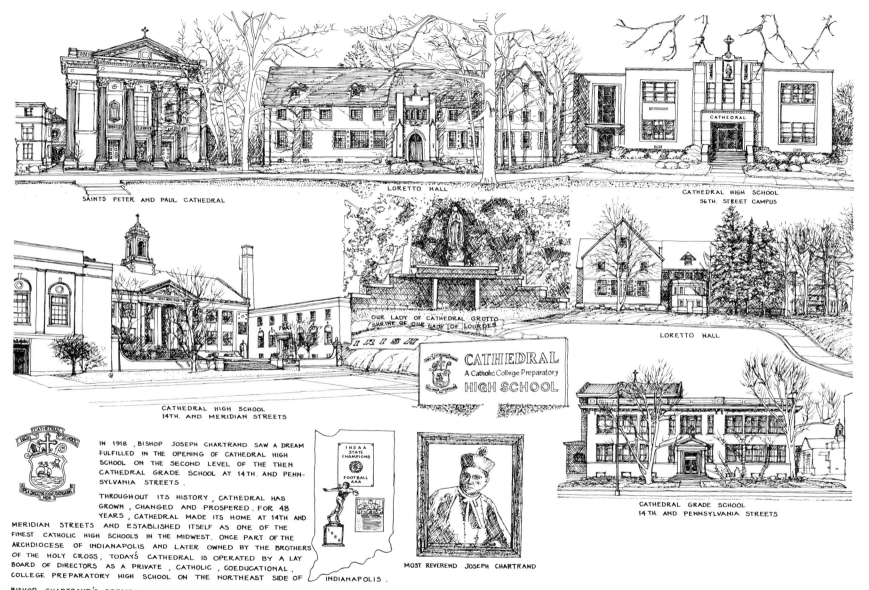

SAINTS PETER AND PAUL CATHEDRAL

LORETTO HALL

CATHEDRAL HIGH SCHOOL
56TH. STREET CAMPUS

OUR LADY OF CATHEDRAL GROTTO
SHRINE OF OUR LADY OF LOURDES

LORETTO HALL

CATHEDRAL HIGH SCHOOL
14TH. AND MERIDIAN STREETS

CATHEDRAL
A Catholic College Preparatory
HIGH SCHOOL

CATHEDRAL GRADE SCHOOL
14TH. AND PENNSYLVANIA STREETS

IN 1918, BISHOP JOSEPH CHARTRAND SAW A DREAM FULFILLED IN THE OPENING OF CATHEDRAL HIGH SCHOOL ON THE SECOND LEVEL OF THE THEN CATHEDRAL GRADE SCHOOL AT 14TH. AND PENNSYLVANIA STREETS.

THROUGHOUT ITS HISTORY, CATHEDRAL HAS GROWN, CHANGED AND PROSPERED. FOR 48 YEARS, CATHEDRAL MADE ITS HOME AT 14TH AND MERIDIAN STREETS AND ESTABLISHED ITSELF AS ONE OF THE FINEST CATHOLIC HIGH SCHOOLS IN THE MIDWEST. ONCE PART OF THE ARCHDIOCESE OF INDIANAPOLIS AND LATER OWNED BY THE BROTHERS OF THE HOLY CROSS, TODAY'S CATHEDRAL IS OPERATED BY A LAY BOARD OF DIRECTORS AS A PRIVATE, CATHOLIC, COEDUCATIONAL, COLLEGE PREPARATORY HIGH SCHOOL ON THE NORTHEAST SIDE OF INDIANAPOLIS.

MOST REVEREND JOSEPH CHARTRAND

BISHOP CHARTRAND'S DREAM LIVES ON AS CATHEDRAL REMAINS A HIGH SCHOOL BUILT ON ACADEMIC EXCELLENCE AND ATHLETIC PROWESS....A HIGH SCHOOL PREPARING LEADERS FOR THE CHURCH AND COMMUNITY.... A HIGH SCHOOL FROM EVERY GEOGRAPHICAL, ECONOMIC, SOCIAL, RACIAL AND RELIGIOUS STRATA OF INDIANAPOLIS AND CENTRAL INDIANA.

CATHEDRAL HIGH SCHOOL EXISTS AS THE DREAM OF YESTERDAY, THE REALITY OF TODAY AND THE PROMISE FOR TOMORROW.

Cathedral High School
Indianapolis, Indiana

Kanwal Prakash Singh
February 1990

CATHEDRAL HIGH SCHOOL Indianapolis, Indiana

STEWART MANOR

FREDERIC M. AYRES AUDITORIUM

FOSTER HALL

PARK·TUDOR SCHOOL

THE CREEK — COLD SPRINGS CAMPUS

UPPER SCHOOL BUILDING

ALLEN W. CLOWES COMMONS

PARK SCHOOL INTRAMURAL BUILDING

FISHER HALL

TUDOR HALL — 32ND. AND MERIDIAN STREETS

PARK-TUDOR SCHOOL, WITH ITS ENROLLMENT OF OVER 690 BOYS AND GIRLS, HAS ITS ROOTS IN TWO INDIANAPOLIS PROPRIETARY SCHOOLS THAT SUBSEQUENTLY BECAME NOT-FOR-PROFIT INSTITUTIONS. IN 1902 FREDONIA ALLEN ESTABLISHED TUDOR HALL SCHOOL AT MERIDIAN AND SIXTEENTH STREETS, AND A DOZEN YEARS LATER WENDELL BROOKS FOUNDED THE BROOK SCHOOL FOR BOYS AT SIXTEENTH AND CENTRAL. TUDOR HAVING OUTGROWN ITS PREMISES BY 1917, MISS ALLEN MOVED HER SCHOOL TO MERIDIAN AND THIRTY-SECOND. IN 1920, FAR-SEEING FATHERS OF THE BOYS PLACED THE BROOK SCHOOL UNDER THE MANAGEMENT OF A BOARD OF DIRECTORS AND CHANGED ITS NAME, FIRST TO BOY'S PREPARATORY SCHOOL AND THEN, AFTER THE SCHOOL'S REMOVAL TO COLD SPRING ROAD, TO PARK SCHOOL.

IN HER WILL MISS ALLEN, WHO DIED IN 1927 COMMITTED THE PERPETUATION OF TUDOR TO A BOARD OF TRUSTEES, WHICH IN 1931 NAMED I. HILDA STEWART PRINCIPAL. HER LABORS WERE CROWNED IN 1959 BY TUDOR'S BUILDING A NEW SCHOOL NORTH OF THE PARK CAMPUS. THE NEIGHBORS, AKIN IN SPIRIT AND AIMS, BECAME ONE SCHOOL IN 1970, OWING TO THE GIFT OF THE FAMILY ORCHARD BY ELI AND J.K. LILLY, JR. MISSES ALLEN AND STEWART, LIKE PARK'S C.O.PAGE AND G.M. GARRETT, SHARED A VISION OF A COLLEGE PREPARATORY SCHOOL SECOND TO NONE IN SCHOLASTIC ACCOMPLISHMENT — A VISION THAT STILL INFORMS PARK TUDOR.

Park-Tudor School, Indianapolis, Indiana

Banwar P. Singh
august 1981

Learning and Discovery

For each of us, there still are worlds to explore, mysteries to solve, mountains to climb, successes to celebrate, and trials to face. Life is a continuous journey of discovery, surprises and encounters, demanding commitments, and spontaneous responses. We struggle to unravel the meaning of life. We hope for better prospects and promising destinations.

We are not alone. We are part of a community of diverse cultures, ideas, and ideals. We have much to learn from and teach each other, and so we must treat each other with consideration and dignity. We must recognize our unique individual spirit, strengths, and collective destiny as fellow travelers in the caravan of life. Along the way, significant experiences contribute to our knowledge and understanding of our universe and awaken our mind and spirit to new possibilities. Let us imagine the impossible. Seek, discover, and welcome ideas that best define our own destinations and serve the greater good of all living beings.

Administration Building
University of Notre Dame

UNIVERSITY OF NOTRE DAME *Notre Dame, Indiana*

CHURCH - LADY OF LORETTO

HOLY CROSS HALL

CENTER BUILDING

LIBRARY

LEMANS HALL DOORWAY

ORIGINALLY STARTED AS A HIGH SCHOOL
ACADEMY **SAINT MARY'S** WAS FOUNDED BY FOUR SISTERS WHO TRAVELLED FROM FRANCE TO
A SMALL COMMUNITY IN SOUTHERN MICHIGAN. THE COLLEGE LATER MOVED TO NOTRE DAME AND
BECAME A PART OF THE EDUCATIONAL COMMUNITY THAT INCLUDES UNIVERSITY OF NOTRE DAME
AND HOLY CROSS JUNIOR COLLEGE.
SAINT MARY'S 275-ACRE CAMPUS IS LOCATED NORTH OF SOUTH BEND, INDIANA. THE 1700
MEMBER STUDENT BODY IS COMPRISED OF WOMEN FROM 48 STATES AND 26 FOREIGN
COUNTRIES. **SAINT MARY'S** OFFERS PROGRAMS LEADING TO BACHELOR OF
ARTS, SCIENCE, FINE ARTS, BUSINESS ADMINISTRATION AND MUSIC. THE
COLLEGE OFFERS STUDY PROGRAMS AT ITS ROME CAMPUS AND AT
SAINT PATRICK'S COLLEGE IN MAYNOOTH, IRELAND. A COOPERATIVE
PROGRAM WITH UNIVERSITY OF NOTRE DAME ENABLES **SAINT MARY'S** STUDENTS TO STUDY IN ANGERS, FRANCE;
INNSBRUCK, AUSTRIA; MEXICO CITY, MEXICO AND TOKYO, JAPAN.
SAINT MARY'S COLLEGE IS ONE OF THE OLDEST CATHOLIC COLLEGE FOR WOMEN IN THE UNITED STATES AND MAINTAINING A TRADITION OF ACADEMIC EXCEL-
LENCE AND DISTINCTIVE EDUCATIONAL OPPORTUNITY SINCE 1844.

Sanwar P. Singh
JANUARY 1980
Sanwar P. Singh

SAINT MARY'S COLLEGE *Notre Dame, Indiana*

HAWA MAHAL

Jaipur, India

HOMES *with* HISTORY

Our home is our castle whether it is a modest dwelling or a beautiful mansion. Our home is a place rich in spirit and personal memories. When the home belongs to a great artist, inventor, educator, writer, emancipator, or leader, then that home takes on an aura of a public attraction and intrigue. Such a home acquires major significance and a sense of history.

We wonder how the people lived and what special elements surrounded their world and environment. We attempt to learn about the lifestyles of prominent figures and understand the lives and spirit of people we admire. We search for some deeper connection in each facet of famous lives as we try to fathom the source of their greatness, gifts, and presence in our lives.

Homes of prominent people are centers of inspiration. Studying their spirit through the images of their lives and legacy, we search for special messages for our times. The drawings in this section represent some homes that are symbols of community pride and heritage.

THE WHITE HOUSE *Washington, D.C.*

In the Stillness of the Morning

In the stillness of early mornings, we sometimes muse in silence. I quietly meditate and search for answers to my personal concerns and about the meaning and mysteries of Life. In this dream-like state, my thoughts often turn toward the unseen realms, the cosmos revealed in scriptures. The Hubble telescope surprised us with an awesome glimpse of our galaxy. We sometimes visit another lifetime or relive memories of our loved ones from whom we are separated by death or circumstance. My mind searches the quadrants of heaven that may be the final destination of my beloved parents. My thoughts, suspended between time and space, drift outside my comfort boundaries into unfamiliar landscapes. They rush toward secret rendezvous, hoping for some spiritual encounter. My spirit sees unique perspectives on life after each such

W.C. Culbertson· Mansion - 1860
New Albany Indiana
Classic Franco - American, Mid-Victorian Style

W.C. CULBERTSON MANSION   *New Albany, Indiana*

experience. My doubts and confusion stay with me when I return to reality.

The messages and connections of such experiences to our present life and circumstances are not always clear. We often wonder about our "journey" into new frontiers. We do not understand their true significance for our lives. Are they reminders, reinforcements, premonitions, or warnings of some sort? We recall the parade of thoughts, people, places, and images blazing past the "window" of our mind toward undefined horizons. These images appear and disappear in an unpredictable dance of hide-and-seek. They tease our mind and spirit. Could these sights and sounds be inspired by some previous-life encounter or foretell a future event?

Our responses vary. We may experience sadness, ecstasy, or stunned disbelief. We may suddenly

1945

श्री पुष्कर राज मेटल्स की रसीद यहां से प्राप्त करें

Bathing Ghats - Pushkar Lake - Pushkar. Rajasthan
One of the holiest places of pilgrimage in India

Banwar P. Singh
april 1977

BATHING GHATS - PUSHKAR *Rajasthan, India*

remember long forgotten events in surprising details. Something ordinary may trigger an avalanche of past memories and emotions. We may uncover a new harvest of precious surprises and reminders. Such unexpected experiences may intrigue our senses and intellect.

With each passing year, the haunting memories of my childhood have become more vivid and alive, the future more uncertain, and the present always full of surprises and annoyances. There perhaps are some special messages for my future in these imaginings and excursions into my childhood experiences. Maybe, I am not supposed to forget the horrors and tragedy of the Partition of India, my family's miraculous escape unscathed, my father's struggles for survival, and his many sacrifices toward my last four decades in America. I could not have imagined the enormity of my blessings when I was passing through those times. My past often reminds me how fortunate I am.

My mind and spirit are swept along in these reflections. My thoughts jump across known and unfamiliar dimensions and long-forgotten thresholds. Then, with a sudden jolt, I awaken to the song and noise of this world. My mind returns from the idle, fanciful, and emotionally charged wanderings to the reality around me. I realize that I am still "on-call" to the demands and promise of my life. I know that I must overcome the shock and challenge of yesterday and look to the future.

The Haimbaugh Barn - Rochester
Fulton County, Indiana

October 1977

HAIMBAUGH BARN *Fulton County, Indiana*

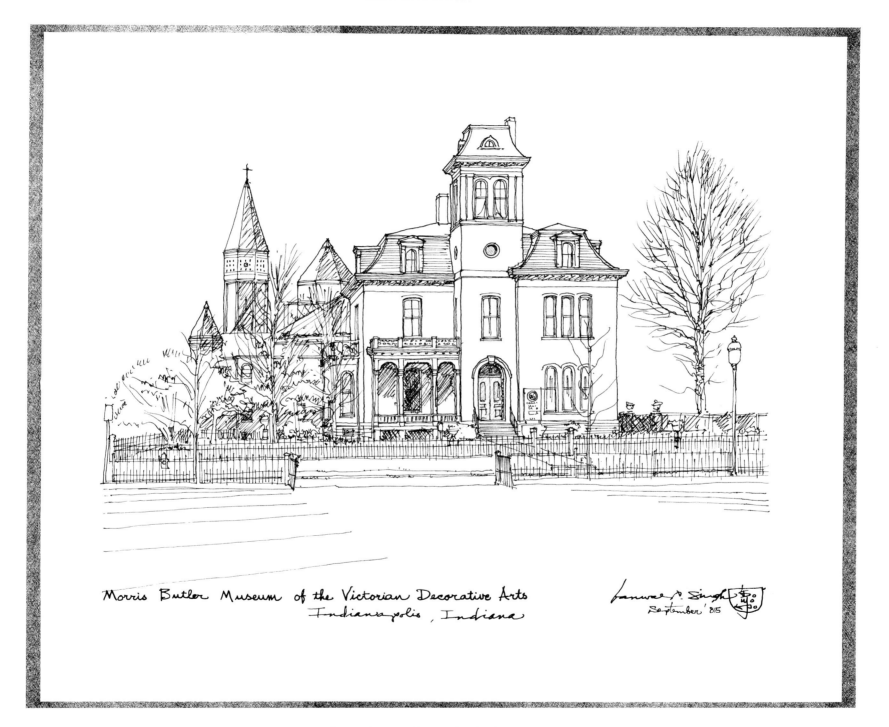

Morris Butler Museum of the Victorian Decorative Arts
Indianapolis, Indiana

Sanwar P. Singh
September '85

MORRIS BUTLER HOME *Indianapolis, Indiana*

To steady and bring "home" my spirit, I recite special prayers, repeat sacred Sikh hymns. I meditate and visualize. Inspiring and beautiful thoughts echo in my mind; I petition in silence:

Lord, make me ready for this day,
Bathe me in Thy Light;
Lead me forward to serve and learn.
Guide my hand to share Thy entrusted gifts
All along the path for my life.
Then, with patience and humility, I wait at Thy Gate;
Receive Thy Command, for my tomorrow.

We wonder and wait for God's Will to unfold, lead us on our journey, and reveal the meaning and purpose in our lives. The Master guards this mystery until it is our time. I must welcome the day before me. Ideas and hopes can use some sunshine.

Windridge Manor, Indianapolis

WINDRIDGE MANOR *Indianapolis, Indiana*

Charleston's beautiful and historic Magnolia Plantation and the world famous gardens are located on the scenic Ashley River. Settled by the Drayton family of England over three centuries ago, the Plantation today is on the National Register of Historic Places. The present house dates from post Civil War.

Magnolia Plantation (about 1671)
Charleston, South Carolina

Kanwar Prakash Singh.
© 2001

THE CHARLES J. KUHN HOUSE WAS BUILT IN 1879. HISTORIC LANDMARKS FOUNDATION RESCUED AND MOVED THE HOUSE TO ITS PRESENT SITE IN 1984 FROM ITS ORIGINAL LOCATION ACROSS THE CANAL AT 431 WEST MICHIGAN STREET. THE KUHN HOUSE WAS LISTED IN THE NATIONAL REGISTER OF HISTORIC PLACES IN 1989. HISTORIC LANDMARKS BEGAN RESTORATION AND NEW CONSTRUCTION THAT MORE THAN DOUBLED ITS SIZE IN MAY 1990. THE WORK WAS COMPLETED IN JANUARY 1991. THE BUILDING WAS OCCUPIED BY HISTORIC LANDMARKS FOUNDATION AS INDIANA'S HERITAGE PRESERVATION CENTER ON FEBRUARY 1, 1991.

HERITAGE PRESERVATION CENTER
State Headquarters of
HISTORIC LANDMARKS FOUNDATION OF INDIANA

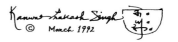

© March 1992

CHATEAU CHAMBORD *Loire Valley, France*

DESIGNED BY H.T. BRANDT , THE 16-ROOM BRICK ITALIANATE MANSION WAS BUILT IN 1875 BY BRIG. GENERAL
BENJAMIN HARRISON, (1833-1901). GEN. HARRISON LATER SERVED AS U.S. SENATOR FROM INDIANA AND WAS
ELECTED PRESIDENT OF THE UNITED STATES IN 1888 .
TODAY THE MANSION IS DESIGNATED AS A NATIONAL HISTORIC LANDMARK AND IS A MEMORIAL TO THE
23RD. PRESIDENT OF THE UNITED STATES OF AMERICA .

President Benjamin Harrison Home
Indianapolis , Indiana

Kanwal Prakash Singh
August 20, 1988

PRESIDENT BENJAMIN HARRISON HOME *Indianapolis, Indiana*

Diamonds in the Grass

As I looked out of the front door, the morning sun had just risen above the rooftops, and its soft light filtered through the trees. The advancing light in the eastern sky lent its magical kiss to the dewdrops scattered overnight on the grass. This gentle encounter gave birth to a glistening carpet of tiny diamonds scattered across the grassy lawn in some mysterious cosmic dance.

For one moment, a celestial splendor seemed to have descended on "my" patch of the earth. The beauty of Nature was being revealed in wonderful ways, at countless places all across Mother Earth. This was nature's salutation, a prayerful offering to the Supreme Creator.

My spirit began to soar. My mind reached upward, imagining the unseen and unfathomable. I was convinced that the heavens must be beautiful beyond description and human imagination. The Sikh scriptures and other sacred texts offer glimpses of the celestial splendor. I began to recite those passages from the Sikh prayer that reveal and celebrate the glory of the Lord's Mansion.

My thoughts returned to earth and the transient nature of life. I began to wonder: the sun will soon gather nature's tiny diamonds spread before me

LILLY PAVILLION *Indianapolis, Indiana*

and will take them away on the sunbeams to some distant horizon. Then they were gone. "All that we see in nature is short-lived and transitory," states the Sikh scriptures, much like "the passing cloud and the dream in the night." God also spirits away our loved ones, often too soon and untimely and invites them to realms beyond our reach and imagination. God never fails to amaze and assure us as He folds and unfolds the cycles of life and the wonders of His Creation. Each experience leaves precious imprints on our mind and spirit before departing. The cherished images of our experiences form the foundation of human imagination. Through them, we discover new meanings about life.

When the sun traveled higher in the sky, it stretched a golden carpet over lands and trails and across unseen horizons. The souls of our loved ones, too, must blaze new trails, find new places to rest, and serve new kingdoms in accordance with a higher command. This is a reassuring thought. Man has found strength in each real or imagined blessing, remembering that the Heavenly Father placed that image and thought before us.

Old Elsie Sweeny Mansion
Columbus Indiana

Ganwad P. Singh

1972

Enlightened Encounters

KEMPER HOUSE *Indianapolis, Indiana*

A special spirit guides the passage of the divinely blessed souls that we may encounter during our earthly journey. They offer us an extraordinary example by their lives, messages, and works. We may not always understand the full measure of their wisdom. Only blessed grace may help us to recognize the truth and light before us.

When a diamond is still in the rough, it does not allow light to penetrate deeply and unmask its full brilliance. Our untrained eye may pass it as an ordinary rock. With our vision clouded by doubt and ignorance, we are unable to see beyond the surface to the limitless riches. We cannot grasp fully the beauty of enlightened souls among us. It is outside our experience. We lack the insight to recognize their true worth and uniqueness and the courage to embrace the unseen and unusual on faith alone. We must search and see to believe.

Fortunately, our encounters with Light and the enlightened seldom fail to tease our imagination about the marvel that may lie beneath the surface of a true gem. We know that in the hands of an experienced master craftsman, the cutting, shaping, polishing, and careful setting can bring forth exquisite beauty. Similarly, great souls mold our beings with Light and spirit-force and leave their own reflections, color, and imprints. They open our windows to the worlds yet unseen and explored and make them manifest.

Suddenly, we may find the path and direction to our lives. We may discover our true destiny for the very first time and become inspired to give it meaning and shape.

SEIBERLING MANSION - 1890
ARCHITECT : ARTHUR LA BELLE   BUILT BY : MONROE SEIBERLING OF DIAMOND
                                                    PLATE GLASS CO.

STYLE : AMERICAN GOTHIC - COMBINES MANY STYLES - NEO JACOBEAN , ROMANESQUE , GOTHIC , MOORISH . WHEN BUILT , IT WAS
CONSTRUCTED INSIDE A FRAME STRUCTURE TO PREVENT INCLEMENT WEATHER FROM HALTING CONSTRUCTION. IT NOW HOUSES HOWARD COUNTY MUSEUM.

Kokomo, Howard County , Indiana

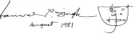

August 1981

James Whitcomb Riley Home
Greenfield Indiana

JAMES WHITCOMB RILEY HOME *Greenfield, Indiana*

Mesa Verde National Park

Mesa Verde National Park, located in S.W. Colorado and established in 1906 covers
an area of 51,333 acres and is famous for well-preserved prehistoric cliff dwellings.

January '79

MESA VERDE NATIONAL PARK, COLORADO

AMBER PALACE

Jaipur, India

TEMPLES *of* JUSTICE

Throughout America, majestic courthouses occupy an important place in county seats. These courthouses symbolize the supreme authority of the laws of the land.

Courthouses are often located in the heart of towns. Businesses, law offices, restaurants, theaters, houses of worship, and other services form the edges of a central square. The masterplan of the town generally follows the classic European tradition of a dominant central anchor, except that the Medieval church as the focal point of the town has been replaced with a courthouse. Over the years, the courthouse squares became special gathering places for community activities and events.

The architectural styles of courthouses greatly vary. We witness innovative adaptations of Romanesque, Greek Revival, Italianate, Second Empire French, Classic, Baroque, Renaissance, Gothic, and other styles and treatments. The structures, domes, and clock towers of the courthouses were visible for miles in the age of the

DECATUR COUNTY COURTHOUSE *Greensburg, Indiana*

horse and wagon. Many of the surviving courthouses date from the later part of the nineteenth century. Statues of county heroes, historic markers, and war relics often grace the facades and grounds of the courthouses. The interiors, with their murals, stained-glass skylights, mosaics, exquisite woodwork, grand marble staircases, fascinating memorabilia, and other surprises provide a unique window to the community spirit and the state of arts and design.

Besides housing the county courts and offices, these beautiful "Temples of Justice" are an important repository of records of the lives, struggles, and history of early settlers. The following pages present drawings of several courthouses in Indiana. The accompanying text offers some thoughts and reflections on the universal hopes and prayers of human beings everywhere: equality, justice, dignity, tolerance, understanding, respect, and sacred human and spiritual rights.

Indiana Courthouses

At the end of the nineteenth century in Indiana and elsewhere, courthouses became symbols of authority, community wealth, and power. There was intense competition among counties about the design and style of their courthouses. To outshine their neighbors and attract prestige and services to their communities, county commissioners invited well-known architects of the times to design and build impressive courthouses. The communities funded and adopted innovative designs and imaginative treatments for their courthouse buildings. Today, the results of

POSEY COUNTY COURTHOUSE *Mount Vernon, Indiana*

their investments and vision are a proud legacy and are enjoyed by the public.

In recent decades, many architectural treasures have been lost due to the need for modern building conveniences, shortsighted policies, real estate pressures, and neglect. Fortunately, thanks to the efforts of local, state, and national historic building trusts, foundations, and preservation groups, the importance of this rich architectural and cultural resource in our communities is beginning to be recognized. Steps are being taken to make our surviving courthouses once again centerpieces of community life.

Old Madison County Court House
Anderson.

Clinton County
Court House
Frankfort

Allen County Court House
Fort Wayne

Johnson County Court House
Franklin

Tiplon
County
Court
House
Tipton

Miami County Court House
Peru

Lake County Court House
Crown Point

Knightstown School
Knightstown

Hancock
County
Court
House
Green-
field

Tippecanoe County
Court House
Lafayette

Cass County Court House
Logansport

Old Marion County Court House
Indianapolis

Morgan County Court House
Martinsville

Decatur County
Court House
Greensburg

Boone County Court House
Lebanon

Hamilton County Court House
Noblesville

Unique and attractive
Court Houses and other
civic structures, repre-
senting many archi-
tectural styles adorn
the city centers of
many communities
across the State of
Indiana.
1973

Indiana Historic Architecture I

Kanwal P. Singh

Common Threads

A nation's history and people shape its culture. Each culture is a unique composite of cherished ideas, ideals, and traditions that in time generate a distinct texture. A culture is a living entity, continuously evolving. Today, these cultural transitions are achieving a global momentum and a new vitality in artistic, architectural, and creative endeavors.

We are discovering that we have much more in common than just similar human emotions, concerns, hopes, and dreams. The emerging cultural mosaics exhibit definite characteristics and connections that suggest common origins.

Many faiths believe that, "God is the Father of all Creation." The Sikh faith proclaimed over five hundred years ago, "O' mortal, Recognize all humanity as One Race, One Brotherhood" for, "Every living being is a repository of the same Divine Light." Now, recent studies of ancient anthropological evidence suggest that it is possible that mankind has a common ancestry; maybe even a single earthly parent going back

CLINTON COUNTY COURTHOUSE *Frankfort, Indiana*

in an unbroken chain of evolution.

The common origin of human beings is an emerging scientific revelation. If proven true, this revolutionary concept can help shatter divisive myths and unjust practices. As a result, a new understanding can emerge affirming that our relationship with our fellow man is more than just spiritual and philosophical but a real sense of a shared life and spirit. How wonderful the very prospect of a single original source!

Many segments of the human cultural tapestry offer reflections of a common unifying spirit and one unmistakable source of all inspirations. Many faiths reason that the threads that bind us to one another stretch directly from One Supreme Creator. Therefore, it is no surprise that we should discover deep emotional and spiritual resonance in human affairs throughout civilization and find strength, comfort, and wisdom in our shared destiny and cultures—a beautiful idea to honor and celebrate!

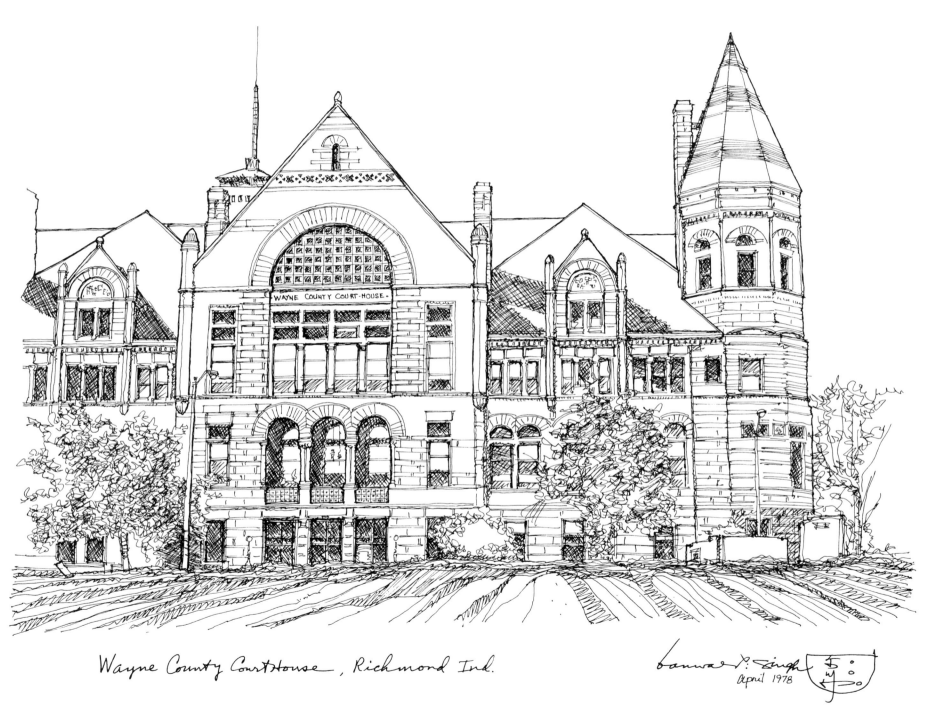

Wayne County CourtHouse, Richmond Ind.

Sanwar P. Singh
April 1978

Montgomery County Court House
Crawfordsville Indiana

MONTGOMERY COUNTY COURTHOUSE *Crawfordsville, Indiana*

Allen County Courthouse - 1897

Fort Wayne, Indiana

Kanwal Prakash Singh
© July 1990

30/40

ALLEN COUNTY COURTHOUSE *Fort Wayne, Indiana*

Building Bridges, Sharing Cultures

The expanding cultural diversity in our midst, though not yet fully discovered or integrated into our community life, is gently introducing new opportunities and transforming the spirit and character of our cities on its own momentum. We can only imagine the response of communities to an open invitation:

Come create a city that reflects the spirit of all people.
Share with us your talents and cultural experiences;
Enrich the emerging "Tapestry of Cultures,"
The sacred Fabric of Faiths
With sounds and splendors of the distant and diverse,
With ideas and ideals that celebrate your heritage and traditions.
Together discover the excitement and echo of our common humanity,
Spirit that unites us as One Universal God's children.
Together shape a legacy that mirrors our shared vision.

Let us make a place at the table for new friends and old,
Share our common dreams and shape a community
Where the Light and the Labors of each one
Enhance the gifts and promise of all.

LAKE COUNTY COURTHOUSE *Crown Point, Indiana*

State Capitol Building , Indianapolis
Built 1888 ; Architetts : Edwin May and Adolf Scherrer

Samuel C. Singh

INDIANA STATE CAPITOL BUILDING *Indianapolis, Indiana*

JOHNSON COUNTY COURTHOUSE *Franklin, Indiana*

New waves of immigrants are converging in America and transplanting their hopes and dreams in our communities. As in the past, immigrants arrive with unique talents, experience, and perspectives. They are eager to work hard and succeed. Our challenge is to transform their amazing energy, deep commitment, special gifts, and skills in building a bright American future. We must assure equal opportunity, continued guidance, and cultural sensitivity to make them responsible and productive citizens.

We must recognize the 'world' around us, bridge cultural differences, reject prejudice, stereotyping, ignorance, and discover the kindred in each other. Indian poet Rabindranath Tagore reminds us that we are all children playing on the seashore of life. We thank our lucky stars that destiny planned this blessed "seashore" as our future home.

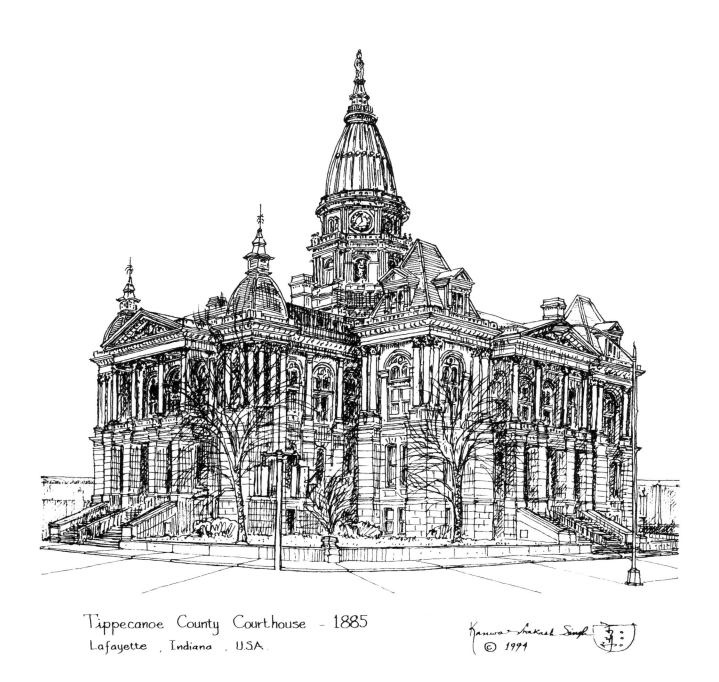

Tippecanoe County Courthouse - 1885
Lafayette , Indiana , U.S.A.

Kanwar Prakash Singh
© 1994

TIPPECANOE COUNTY COURTHOUSE *Lafayette, Indiana*

Orange County Courthouse - 1847-1850
Paoli , Indiana
Greek Revival Style

Kanwal Prakash Singh
© September 1988

In Defense of Rights and Freedom

As an act of our common humanity, we must safeguard the dignity of all God's children. Injury to the civic or spiritual rights of even one soul is an affront to human decency everywhere and to God who loves us all. Inaction on the part of people of goodwill may encourage continued aggression, embolden the oppressor, and repeat the long nightmares of the past. We are reminded by many who stood for human rights that it is an act of faith to stand united in spiritual and human solidarity in the face of evil. The sacrifices of pious souls set before us an example of extraordinary dimension: physical, cultural, and spiritual differences must not stop us from doing the right thing. We must be prepared to cross the temporal and spiritual boundaries to defend the fundamental freedoms and rights of all people.

BOONE COUNTY COURTHOUSE *Lebanon, Indiana*

Imagine crossing and traversing boundaries as a bridge to a more enlightened and peaceful world where unity of purpose, equality of opportunity, sanctity of all faiths, dignity of each individual, and justice for all are enshrined as the "Universal Commandments." No sacrifice is too great to safeguard them, and no one is left outside this universal circle of hope and basic dignity. Sikhs remember the saintly Teg Bahadur, the ninth Sikh Guru, for the ultimate sacrifice of his life in 1675 in defense of universal sacred rights. The United Nations today recognizes him as a great champion of human rights.

The spirit of sacrifice continues to inspire us to create a world where right actions, not fear, shape human destiny, where tolerance and understanding reign supreme. May all of us live the true essence of our sacred texts by respecting the faith of others.

Bartholomew County Courthouse *Columbus, Indiana*

WHITE COUNTY COURTHOUSE AT MONTICELLO WAS DESIGNED BY ARCHITECTS LABELLE AND FRENCH OF MARION INDIANA. IT WAS COMPLETED IN 1895 AT A COST OF $70,000 WITH ANOTHER $30,000 SPENT ON FURNISHINGS. THE MAJESTIC INDIANA LIMESTONE BUILDING STOOD 108 FEET FROM THE GROUND TO THE TOP OF THE TOWER. THE TOWER HELD CLOCKS AND BELLS. THE COURTHOUSE WAS BADLY DAMAGED ON APRIL 3, 1974 AND WAS REPLACED BY A MODERN STRUCTURE.

White County Courthouse (1895–1974)
Monticello, Indiana

Sanwar P. Singh
October 1981

WHITE COUNTY COURTHOUSE *Monticello, Indiana*

Vigo County CourtHouse
Terre Haute Indiana

march 1976

VIGO COUNTY COURTHOUSE *Terre Haute, Indiana*

Ohio County Court House , Rising Sun , Indiana
"Indiana's oldest Court House in continuous use" - 1845

Kanwar Prakash Singh
© August '88

OHIO COUNTY COURTHOUSE *Rising Sun, Indiana*

Bartholomew County CourtHouse – 1874
Columbus, Indiana
Architect : Isaac Hodgson

Sanwal P. Singh
October 1977

Knox County Court House
Vincennes, Indiana

KNOX COUNTY COURTHOUSE *Vincennes, Indiana*

Fayette County Court House
Connersville Indiana

Kanwar C. Singh
September 1978

Fulton County Court House , Rochester, Indiana

Builder/Designer : A.W. Rush and son   Completed : 1895
Architectural Style : Romanesque

June 1979

FULTON COUNTY COURTHOUSE *Rochester, Indiana*

Martin County Courthouse
Shoals, Indiana

Kanwal Prakash Singh
© September 1988

MARTIN COUNTY COURTHOUSE *Shoals, Indiana*

Jasper County Courthouse - 1898
Rensselaer, Indiana

Kanwal Prakash Singh
© 1994

JASPER COUNTY COURTHOUSE *Rensselaer, Indiana*

Reflections on September 11

Union County Courthouse *Liberty, Indiana*

Drowned in a flood of emotion and reflection;
We found strength and healing
In welcome prayers in many traditions,
In boundless acts of selfless generosity,
In embracing hope in the midst of such tragedy.

We overcame some past indifference:
Meeting for the first time on neighborhood streets, interfaith forums,
We discovered beautiful "strangers" in the crowd.
We understood that together we must heal our wounded nation.
We found unexpected strength in each other to carry us forward.

We suddenly saw fellow Americans in a new light:
Most as good and decent people
Tirelessly striving with a spirited pride,
Each shaping cherished hopes and dreams
"Weaving" them into our common national destiny.

Monroe County Court House
Bloomington Indiana

1974

MONROE COUNTY COURTHOUSE *Bloomington, Indiana*

1879 - Wabash County Court House
Wabash, Indiana

WABASH COUNTY COURTHOUSE *Wabash, Indiana*

Our hearts will heal with the passage of time:
Each new day enlarges our awareness of those around us,
A welcome awakening bridges old divides and separations,
A kindred destiny leading us to new friendships
As we rediscover and rebuild our world.

Out of tragedy, a prayerful nation emerges:
Reunited in purpose and standing tall,
Rededicated to precious freedoms and a future
Where no one is outside the circle of basic rights;
Each may serve and shape this sacred promise.

We are mindful of the awesome challenge:
Diversity of ideas, traditions, and perceptions
Forging one vision out of many, honoring all perspectives,
Strengthening the fabric of our shared humanity
Where hope is a birthright and a singular passion.

Such lofty dreams frequently test the human soul:
There will be triumphs and many trials along the way;
Getting there is a vision we can hardly abandon or ignore.
With a renewed and rekindled spirit we must welcome
Our momentous tryst with all tomorrows.

Rush County Court House
Rushville, Indiana

RUSH COUNTY COURTHOUSE *Rushville, Indiana*

Breaking Silence

Lord, break the silence of each morning
with the songs of birds and the sacred music of Thy Praise.

Lift the burdens of blind temptations and selfish pursuits
with reflections of the sacred and a spirit of selfless service.

End the silent sufferings and sorrows of the innocent
with healing thoughts and renewal of spirit.

Dispel the despair, sadness, and unbearable pain of the children
with songs of hope and the dance of dreams.

End the nightmares and traumas that torture humanity
with prayerful healing and the renewal of hope.

Dismantle the walls of prejudice, discrimination, and ignorance of the past
with a new understanding and tolerance of our differences.

Stop the tragic exploitations and trampling of basic liberties
with righteous force and just laws;
stand in solidarity with other voices of reason and conscience.

HAMILTON COUNTY COURTHOUSE *Noblesville, Indiana*

CEILING DETAIL

STAINED GLASS WINDOW

Honorable Judge Steckler
Congratulations for a
distinguished
Service to the State
of Indiana

HON. JUDGE STECKLER'S COURT ROOM - THE OLD "WEST COURTROOM"

BRONZE METAL GATE & RAILING

THE COURTROOM OF THE HONORABLE WILLIAM E. STECKLER IS A STUNNING MONUMENT TO THE MAJESTY OF THE FEDERAL JUDICIARY AND THE COMMON LAW. ORIGINALLY KNOWN AS THE "WEST COURTROOM" OF THE UNITED STATES COURTHOUSE IN INDIANAPOLIS, ARCHITECTS JOHN HALL RANKIN AND THOMAS KELLOGG ACHIEVED THEIR PURPOSE OF CREATING AN ATMOSPHERE OF JUSTICE AND EQUALITY IN A SETTING REMINISCENT OF SIXTEENTH CENTURY ROME.

BEHIND JUDGE STECKLER'S MAHOGANY BENCH IS THE W.B. INGEH PAINTING "THE APPEAL TO JUSTICE". AN INTRICATE BRONZE RAIL SEPARATES THE WELL OF THE COURTROOM FROM THE GALLERY. TWO MAGNIFICENT STAINED GLASS WINDOWS FILL THE COURTROOM WITH A KALEIDOSCOPE OF COLOR THROUGH A PROFUSION OF SCROLLS, BASKETS OF FRUIT, WINGED CHERUBS AND THE SCALES OF JUSTICE. THE COAT OF ARMS OF THE ORIGINAL THIRTEEN STATES DISPLAYED HIGH ABOVE THE COURTROOM PROVIDE A CONSTANT REMINDER OF THE ORIGIN OF OUR REPUBLIC.

Judge William E. Steckler's Courtroom -
United States Courthouse , Indianapolis , Indiana

Kanwar Prakash Singh
December 8, 1986

ELKHART COUNTY COURT HOUSE *Goshen, Indiana*

Eliminate all threats, denials, and suppression of sacred rights
with full recognition and protection of the absolute sanctity of these rights.

Protect us from the mortal dangers that threaten life, liberty, and pursuit of happiness
with strong safeguards that assure freedom, justice, and equal opportunity for all.

Break the cycles of violence, hate, despair, and overwhelming fears
with welcome sunshine, uplifted spirit, and anchors of hope.

Vanquish the silent hidden demons that destroy self-esteem, threaten our well-being;
deepen our sense of hopelessness, rejection, and abandonment
with thoughtful answers, sensitivity, and imaginative safeguards.

End all darkness that causes deep anguish and robs many of their basic humanity
with measures that heal and assure full dignity to each.

Restore and renew our cherished hopes, inspire new dreams
with an enlightened community vision and optimism;
lead each of us toward the fullness of our lives, promise, and destiny.

Meditation:

Every living being is precious: *"A repository of Divine Light"*
Each of us must lead and serve
This is a special privilege.

Let the angel in us guide our spirit:
Teach us prayer songs, sacred chants, dance, music, laughter, and loving
thoughts with a universal echo.
Together, we expand and honor the collective, colorful, and rich tapestry
of our uniqueness;
Let the SUPREME FATHER OF ALL CREATION do the rest.

TIPTON COUNTY COURTHOUSE *Tipton, Indiana*

Blackford County Courthouse - 1893 - 1894
Hartford City, Indiana

Kanwal Prakash Singh
© August 1988

BLACKFORD COUNTY COURTHOUSE *Hartford City, Indiana*

Henry County Court House
New Castle Indiana

Samuel V. Singh
July 1976

HENRY COUNTY COURTHOUSE *New Castle, Indiana*

Spirit and Place

Tippecanoe County Courthouse - 1885
Lafayette, Indiana

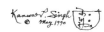

TIPPECANOE COUNTY COURTHOUSE *Lafayette, Indiana*

Imagine a place where there are no closets that hide the countless acts of shame, outrage, and inhumanity that cause suffering to the human spirit. This place is free of assaults on human decency, silent indignities, unprovoked hostility, and crimes against children and the defenseless. Discrimination and prejudice, unjust laws, violations, and denials of fundamental human and sacred rights, and other problems find no sanctuary.

In this place, dignity, freedoms, and civil liberties of each individual are recognized as a sacred trust; the welfare of each citizen is a basic and shared responsibility. This place does not ignore the special needs of any citizen.

In this place, the rule of just laws transcends all divides. This place recognizes the unmistakable universality in the human spirit. There is a growing spirit of unity among people, culture, and faith traditions. Leaders and institutions here honor, strengthen, and celebrate the full spectrum of human talents, creativity, and visions.

HENDRICKS COUNTY
COURT HOUSE

TOWN OF DANVILLE
WELCOMES
PRESIDENT REAGAN

PRESIDENT REAGAN

PRESIDENT REAGAN RECEIVING THE PRINT FROM THE
COUNTY COMMISSIONERS

COURT HOUSE ROTUNDA / INTERIOR

"OUR COUNTRY ... OUR STATE ... OUR COUNTY... OUR TOWN ... WERE ALL
REPRESENTED IN THE ROTUNDA OF THE HENDRICKS COUNTY
COURT HOUSE, DANVILLE, INDIANA, ON JULY 13, 1987 —
A SYMBOL OF FREEDOM, DEMOCRACY AND HOPE
FOR THE FUTURE.
OUR PRESIDENT, RONALD REAGAN, CAME TO OUR TOWN
TO INTRODUCE HIS ECONOMIC BILL OF RIGHTS, STRESSING
FREEDOM TO WORK, TO ENJOY THE FRUITS OF OUR LABOR, TO
OWN AND TO CONTROL OUR PROPERTY AND TO PARTICIPATE IN
THE FREE MARKET.
OUR GOVERNOR, ROBERT D. ORR, VISITED OUR TOWN, TOO. HE
WITNESSED OUR COUNTY COMMISSIONERS, HERSHEL A. GENTRY JR.,
M. RICHARD HIMSEL AND RAYMOND E. ANDREWS,
PRESENT A PRINT OF AN ORIGINAL PEN AND INK DRAWING OF HENDRICKS COUNTY
LANDMARKS TO OUR PRESIDENT.
HISTORY WAS MADE FOR DANVILLE AS PEOPLE OF ALL AGES WAVED THEIR FLAGS AND HANDS
TO THE PRESIDENTIAL LIMOUSINE AS IT WAS ESCORTED BY MOTORCYCLE POLICEMEN FROM THE
INDIANAPOLIS POLICE DEPARTMENT." — JUDGE JEFFREY V. BOLES AND BETTY J. WEESNER.

July 13, 1987 -- A Presidential Visit Remembered

Kanwal Prakash Singh
© July 13, 1988

PRESIDENTIAL VISIT REMEMBERED *Danville, Indiana*

TAJ MAHAL

Agra, India

MONUMENTS *and* MEMORIALS

E VERY COMMUNITY HAS its own proud moments, great heroes, and symbols of achievement. From times immemorial, man has celebrated significant events and contributions with memorials and monuments. Man has often seen these memorials as reminders and symbols of human triumphs, agony, conscience, and greatness.

GATEHOUSE-CROWN HILL CEMETERY *Indianapolis, Indiana*

Our monuments and memorials are diverse in concept, design, and vision. There are countless statues dedicated to saints, warriors, soldiers, kings, and leaders. There are walls of memory, fountains with dancing nymphs, victory columns, towers, piazzas, arches, mausoleums, memorial gardens, libraries, museums, and arcades dedicated to brave souls who blazed new trails and served mankind. Many monuments and memorials combine multiple functions and several structures.

These memorials and monuments celebrate community history and heritage. Monuments and memorials contribute to the beauty of urban environments; many represent great architectural and artistic achievements. The major memorials, with many components and living functions, remind us of our past journey and future promise. Monuments and memorials carry lessons of hope and vision, challenge and inspiration, and beauty and spirit that give character to our community and depth to our humanity. The drawings in this section offer a glimpse of this special feature in our communities.

Lincoln Memorial

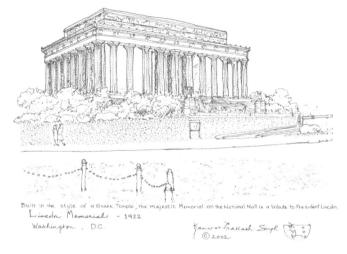

Built in the style of a Greek Temple, the majestic Memorial on the National Mall is a tribute to President Lincoln.

Lincoln Memorial - 1922
Washington, D.C.
Kanwar Prakash Singh
© 2002

LINCOLN MEMORIAL *Washington D.C.*

For me, the Lincoln Memorial in Washington, D.C. evokes intense emotions of reverence, liberty, and sacrifice. The Memorial, dedicated in 1922 to the sixteenth President of the United States, Abraham Lincoln, is a majestic presence at one end of the National Mall in Washington, D.C. The following inscription reminds us that this is hallowed ground:

"In this temple, as in the hearts of the people for whom he saved the Union, the memory of Abraham Lincoln is enshrined forever."

The Memorial represents a turning point in the history of the young Republic. It is dedicated to an enlightened soul, a noble giant, an emancipator, and martyr to the cause of humanity. His life, courage, and wisdom will continue to inspire future generations. The Memorial serves as an enduring symbol of freedom, tolerance, and justice for all Americans. The Memorial also is a favorite gathering place for visitors from many nations.

Designed as a classic Greek Temple, the Memorial symbolizes the unity of the nation with thirty-six Doric columns representing the thirty-six states that existed at the time the Memorial was dedicated.

An 18-foot tall sculpture by Daniel Chester French of a seated Lincoln is in the center of the chamber. Lincoln's famous Gettysburg Address is inscribed on the south wall of the Monument below a mural painted by Jules Guerin depicting the angel of truth freeing a slave. Lincoln's Second Inaugural Address is etched into the north wall below another mural by Guerin that depicts the unity of North and South.

A Landmark - Statue of Liberty , New York
Designed by F. A. Bartholdi in 1884.

STATUE OF LIBERTY *New York City, New York*

Ancient Ruins

The historic ruins at Baalbeck, Lebanon, the Colosseum in Rome, the Parthenon in Athens, the Wailing Wall in Jerusalem, the ancient sites of Mohenjodaro and Harappa in Pakistan, Machu Picchu in Peru, Luxor in Egypt, Angkor Wat in Cambodia, and thousands of other heritage sites "speak" to us as witnesses to past wars, intrigues, triumphs, and tragedies. They display symbols and scars of cultural invasions and architectural transformations in the landscapes of ancient civilizations. Even in their silence, these broken fragments of once-celebrated grandeur take our minds and spirits to times and events of long ago.

Amidst the dates, historical associations, remnants

COLOSSEUM *Rome, Italy*

of art and architectural treasures at these sites, we search for connections with the ancient past. We want to explore the inspirations, imagination, daring, and traditions of those who have gone before and paved the way for us. Today, these architectural ruins are "living" libraries for scholars, students, archeologists, and interested citizens everywhere. Preservation, restoration, and protection of such sites must remain a major commitment.

As pilgrims traveling alone or in modern-day caravans to the important heritage sites and destinations, we come face to face with our architectural past and often discover meaningful thresholds, surprising insights, and new inspirations for our future.

OLD CHICAGO WATER TOWER AND PUMPING STATION WERE THE ONLY PUBLIC BUILDINGS THAT SURVIVED THAT GREAT CHICAGO FIRE OF 1871. THIS CITY LANDMARK WAS BUILT IN 1869 IN CASTELLATED GOTHIC STYLE BY WILLIAM W. BOYINGTON - A PROMINENT CHICAGO ARCHITECT.

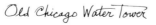

OLD CHICAGO WATER TOWER *Chicago, Illinois*

Taj Mahal

The Taj Mahal gives the city of Agra, India, a sense of identity and a proud association with an architectural wonder. The Taj offers the world an icon of magnificence and enshrines the universal human emotion of love.

The exquisite jeweled inlay work throughout the tomb, built by Moghul Emperor Shahjehan in memory of his Queen Mumtaz Mahal, has been described as "designed by the giants and finished by the jewelers." The great Indian poet Rabindranath Tagore described the beauty of the Taj as "a tear on the face of eternity."

Imagine 20,000 people working under the direction of the most accomplished craftsmen from many countries for over twenty-two years, completing the

Taj Mahal, Agra - 1653

TAJ MAHAL *Agra, India*

Taj Mahal in 1653. The white marble came from a quarry in Rajasthan, and the precious stones were brought from many lands to give shape to the Emperor's vision of love: perfection, grandeur, and unsurpassed beauty. A formal Moghul garden in front and the River Yamuna in the back add to the charm and fabulous setting of the Taj.

In the Taj, art and architecture have created a "living" marvel in marble and precious stones, a true symphony of sensual charm that offers heavenly reflections in the mirrors of mind and human spirit. The Taj, as a monument to the creative genius of man, transports our imagination to new highs in building arts. It is the crown jewel of the great architectural legacy that belongs to the ages.

The Taj Mahal (1632-53) in Agra, India, the most famous example of Indo-Islamic architecture, is the mausoleum which the Moghul Emperor Shah Jehan erected for his favorite wife, Mumtaz Mahal. The Taj represents the brightest jewel of many built during the Golden Age of Moghul Architecture.

Moghul Emperor Shah Jehan's Taj Mahal (1632-53) Agra, India

TAJ MAHAL Agra, India

Memories, Heritage, and Legacy

Our memories link us with our past; we speak and sometimes live through them. Arts, architecture, archeology, and our creative treasures evoke special memories of the human journey and experiences through the ages. Our heritage is a composite of our cherished cultural, spiritual, and creative treasures. Heritage is shaped by unique human challenges and reflects the character, accomplishments, and spirit of the community, culture, and civilization of its origin. Architectural, artistic, and cultural heritage provides a window and insights into the past and new understanding and inspirations for the future. Today, we think of humanity's rich legacy as the collective heritage of mankind.

Our legacy, on the other hand, represents a unique human component. It refers to the special ancestral gifts bequeathed to us by law or association. Our legacy offers special reflections of our pursuits and endeavors, trials and triumphs, and other ideas

Archdiocese of Indianapolis
The Catholic Church in Indiana
(1834 - 1984)

SAINT MARY-OF-THE KNOBS, INDIANA

and ideals that define our vision, strengths, and character. Legacy is a measure of the life, spirit, and gifts of generations past. Legacy may be our own unique inheritance, but we share its common rewards and inspirations with others around us and with all humanity.

Architecture is a record of the turns and twists of history. It reflects the emergence of new styles and forms and revolutionary advancements in building technology. Architecture provides us with tangible evidence of the changes in society over the centuries; it offers a record of the renaissance in thought and spirit and the state of the arts. Throughout history, architecture employed the latest creative and imaginative advantages to improve and dramatize the existing "orders" and shaped new recognizable identity in style and character that best defined the times and society.

Recoleta Cemetery &
Basilica of Nuestra Señora del Pilar - 1732 (Background)
Buenos Aires, Argentina

Kanwar Prakash Singh
© 2003

Cherished Blessings

Oh heart, ache not for things thou cannot change;
Ask not, nor long for
Rewards thou cannot rightly claim,
Nor in temptation cherish
What rightly belongs to thy neighbor.
Seek not in envy, nor in anger rob
The rightful blessings and sunshine of others
Sharing thy journey and passage in life.

Let thy gifts and labors anchor thy voyage;
With treasures thou has earned and shared
Discover thy true destiny.
With an unbound spirit, follow the stars of promise
Shape daily new temples of service to the living.
Dignify and honor life;
Find new rewards mirrored all around.

LINCOLN BOYHOOD NATIONAL MEMORIAL *Lincoln City, Indiana*

MONUMENT CIRCLE *Indianapolis, Indiana*

BOATS OFF
BOMBAY
India

NATURE, INSPIRATION, *and* CREATIVITY

NATURE IS A LIMITLESS SOURCE OF WONDER and inspiration, of beauty, reflections, innovations, and colorful creations. Nature offers us a glimpse of the mysteries in creation, the grandeur of countless galaxies and stars strung across space. Nature offers us affirmations of a divine spirit radiating across the living landscapes and unseen sacred realms. Nature greatly enhances our awareness of our own temporal universe.

Nature is a unique classroom where we can experience a broad spectrum of life's richness and splendor. Nature enshrines invaluable lessons, each encounter revealing new secrets and opening new windows to the world around us. Nature is a symbol of divine power, mystery, benevolence, and change. It is a boundless source of gifts to sustain, nurture, strengthen, and enhance life. Nature is a sanctuary for learning, renewal, and communion with our deeper self.

Nature is a source of inspiration to life, spirit, and creativity. Every falling snowflake, glistening dewdrop, bird in flight, gust of wind, passing cloud, and rainstorm with bolts of lightning carries an unmistakable message. Every challenge in Nature and flights of our imagination test our will and define our limits, possibilities, and responses. Countless sights and sounds in nature contribute to designs, patterns, motifs, rhythms, expressions, and innovations to serve life.

Nature is an incredible force for change. Nature dares us to discover and embrace bold new ideas and innovations, fashion new designs and creations, conquer great challenges, and enrich and advance human civilization. Understanding, conservation, and preservation of our environment are essential to finding true peace and future happiness. The text in this section offers some musings about the beauty and splendor of nature. I also share other inspirations that challenge my hopes, imagination, and spirit.

Sharing God's Light

Lord, may Thy Light radiate from every living being,
The whole Earth may glow in Thy warmth and radiance;
Darkness all around, bathed in Light, may be spirited away.
Thy Creation may revel in goodness for a brief moment.

Lord, inspire and lead us to do our part:

With a prayerful spirit, in Salutation and celebration,
Make daily offerings of special gifts at Thy Sacred Altars.
Serve and expand hope with the all Thou has entrusted;
Witness Thy Living Wonders all around.

Krannert Trust Philanthropic Legacy   Kanwal Prakash Singh — April 1988

INDIANAPOLIS ZOO *Indianapolis, Indiana*

Arts and Spirituality

Throughout history, the arts have interpreted and reflected the essence of life, culture, and spirit of nations. Arts take our imaginations to the farthest reaches of the seen and unseen temporal and celestial mystery and splendor. Arts take their inspirations from human adventure and experience as well as from the revelations in sacred texts and inspired literature. Master builders, craftsmen, and artists give such knowledge dramatic physical forms and visual expressions to transport our minds and senses to the realms of pleasure, awe, inspiration, and devotion. Their grand visions and creations often carry deep imprints of the spirit of the masters themselves.

Architecture as a fine art is unique. It combines many art forms. Beautiful architecture is the principle focus of my interest and artwork. I attempt to capture the spirit of special buildings and sites in my drawings and preserve them on paper. Through my drawings, I

MISS VICTORY STATUE, *Indianapolis, Indiana*

rediscover a community's architectural legacy, the rich composite of styles, traditions, and artistic details in landmark buildings. I explore and understand the culture, faith, and ideals that inspired their designs, embellishments, and aesthetics. A brief history of the buildings is often a design element in my composite drawings.

Historic buildings must have a special and honored place as community cultural sites. They represent community arts, culture, history, and heritage. Through my artwork and writings, I advocate the preservation and restoration of significant architecture. When feasible, we must adapt such a resource to new and innovative uses instead of destroying it. Communities must adopt and enact guidelines that safeguard and encourage the careful integration of major architectural sites and attractions into the emerging fabric of our towns and cities.

The drawings in this book introduce people to the special architectural treasures from many places. They invite the viewer to explore, experience, and enjoy the beauty of special structures and sites around them. The images present striking highlights, building and sculptural details, and inspirations behind the outstanding edifice or site to send the spirit on a journey of further discovery and learning.

Fortunately, some of these landmarks have survived the ravages of times and stand before us in splendor and beauty. It is up to us to guard them. Their legacy affirms the divine in their endeavors and continues to remind us of our urgent challenge. We must preserve this resource for future generations. We know that special architectural sites give a community a sense of place, identity, character, and charm. We cherish beauty, history, and symbolism in our environment.

Arts: architecture, literature, and music can be a major force for good. These and other arts that reinforce and echo broad precepts and exude a positive cultural and spiritual energy can transcend the entire spectrum of the diverse and unfamiliar. Arts can be a powerful source of learning, appreciating, and understanding the nature of Man and his universe. Arts can be the foundation of human unity in spirit, our cultural bridge to one another. Our diverse faiths shape our ideas and ideals, but spirituality and inspirations reverberate with many shared interests and purpose. We discover common ground in the beauty in nature, wonderful artistic creations, and universal human emotions.

My faith, spirit, and spirituality are never far from my artwork. For me, the matters of spirit are the essence of life itself. Spirituality is a vital dimension of humanity. Our inspiration, understanding, and commitment define our spirituality; our faith gives our creativity texture and spirit. My artwork and writings reflect my faith, traditions, and spirituality. My faith commands and advocates equality, justice, human dignity, sanctity of all life, and sacred traditions, the preservation and enhancement of the human environment, and uplifting the human spirit with all the gifts that are temporarily entrusted to us. My art honors, communicates, and celebrates that spirit and message.

HISTORIC MOSQUE *Ajmer, India*

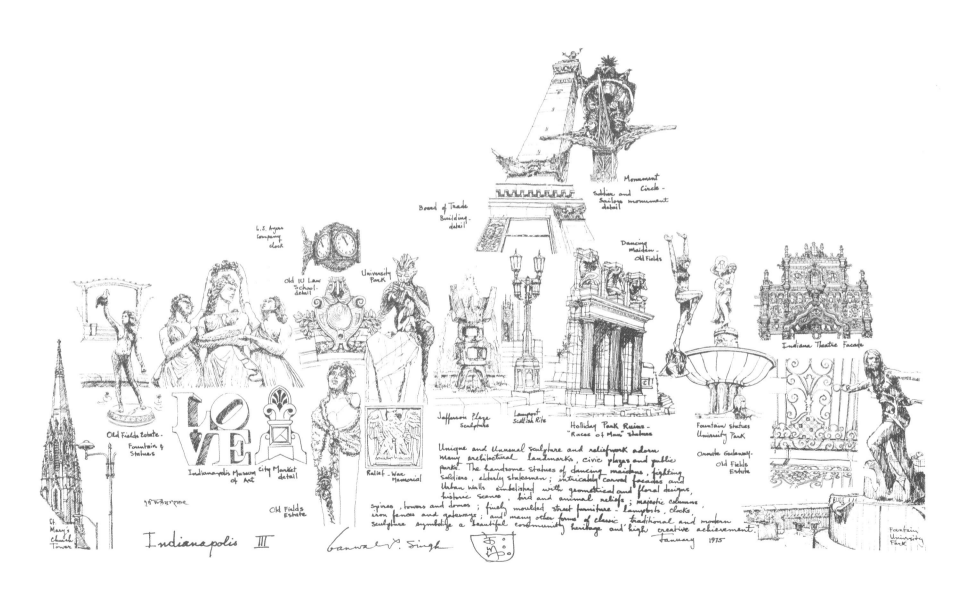

Monument Circle -
Soldier and
Sailors monument
detail

Board of Trade
Building
detail

L. S. Ayers
Company
clock

Dancing
Maiden -
Old Fields

Old IU Law
School -
detail

University
Park

Indiana Theatre Facade

Old Fields Estate -
Fountain & Statues

LOVE

Jefferson Plaza
Sculpture

Lampost
Scottish Rite

Holliday Park Ruins -
"Races of Man" statues

Fountain Statues
University Park

Indianapolis Museum
of Art

City Market
detail

Relief - War
Memorial

Ornate Gateway -
Old Fields
Estate

Unique and unusual sculpture and reliefwork adorn
many architectural landmarks, civic plazas and public
parks. The handsome statues of dancing maidens, fighting
soldiers, elderly statesmen; intricately carved facades and
urban walls embelished with geometrical and floral designs,
historic scenes, bird and animal reliefs; majestic columns,
spires, towers and domes; finely moulded street furniture - lamposts, clocks
iron fences and gateways; and many other forms of classic traditional and modern
sculpture symbolize a beautiful community heritage and high creative achievement.

Old Fields
Estate

St. Mary's
Church
Tower

Indianapolis III

Kanwal S. Singh

January 1975

Fountain
University
Park

Sikh Prayer that Longs for a World at Peace

Ardas, the closing prayer in the Sikh worship tradition, ends with a universal blessing for all humanity: "By thy grace, may there be peace and goodwill among all people everywhere." Sikh scriptures remind us to understand and celebrate our common humanity.

Peace and goodwill are an important condition for human survival and progress. A state of peace must prevail for "life, liberty, and the pursuit of happiness" and for communion with our deeper self. A spirit of friendship and goodwill among nations and people can "make the world kin." Conflicts erupt, discords arise when a civilized society fails to guarantee freedom, justice, civilized dignity, and equal opportunity to all citizens.

The task of finding new solutions to old and new universal challenges, building bridges of trust and lasting peace among nations, faiths, and ethnic communities remains an unrealized hope. Poverty, hunger, injustice, illiteracy, and divisiveness dominate global concerns.

I have meditated upon the words of the great Indian sage and humanitarian Rabindranath Tagore's moving and enlightened writings, especially Gitanjali, for which he won a Nobel Prize in literature in 1913. I offer my prayer for a world at peace, drawing inspiration from my faith, struggles, experiences, and the echoes of Tagore's hauntingly beautiful prayer songs.

CHRIST CHURCH CATHEDRAL -1860

CHRIST CHURCH CATHEDRAL

Peace that: transcends temporal frontiers,
Reaches deep into the spiritual realm,
Transports our spirit to a new purpose,
Sets our sight to a higher promise.

Peace that: accepts all triumph and trials,
Inspires respect and understanding among nations,
Discovers meaning and challenge in all things,
Entertains the good of all Creation.

Peace where: the threat of war is a distant memory,
Peaceful coexistence is not an illusion,
Unwelcome conflicts do not intrude on human space,
Might surrenders to right in loving grace.

Peace where: the mind captures and honors the essence of life,
The soul dances to the rhythms of universal joy,
Great ideas are rewarded and celebrated,
Common everyday living is a cherished pastime.

Peace where: the heart cherishes giving,
Giving in faith is a sacred rite,
The true count of blessings begins with giving,
The spirit yearns to serve as an offering.

Peace where: legends and tradition echo and affirm Universal spirit,
Faith and seva (service) converge to mirror our humanity,
The Light of the Unseen guides us through unimagined valleys,
The promise of tomorrows keeps hope and dreams alive.

Peace where: despair and divisiveness no longer threaten the human race,
Ignorance and injustice find no friendly place,
Vision and striving strengthen and thread human destiny,
Diversity of thoughts and ideas is a cherished treasure.

Peace where: reason and truths herald triumphs,
Dignity and justice are sacred rights,
Love transcends all colors and separating walls,
Hope and freedom are an eternal flame.

Lord, teach us to make peace with all that surrounds us. May we reflect on the meaning and shape of our universe and nurture it with prayer, sacrifice, and inspirations of great souls. May our labors and prayers converge to create a beautiful canopy of dignity, equality, justice, and friendship for all living beings under the heavens to live and prosper in peace.

May all creation move forward in solidarity, oneness of spirit and purpose, and together shape and inherit a legacy worthy of God and man, where peace is not a dream but our true destiny.

Time and Again

You take me by the hand past uncertainty and harm:
Dance of death, genocide, roaring waters swirling all around;
You lift me from the valleys of unfriendly shadows,
Bless me to witness Your Grandeur from Himalayan heights.

At every turn You surround me with gifts
Far beyond my labors and imagination,
Your pleasure and power, I cannot fathom.
My temporal limits place your Greatness beyond my wisdom.

I am lost in the maze of Your awesome Majesty and Mystery
Revealed in Song and Spirit by the Great Gurus (Teachers).
Teach me Your Ways; take me O' Father as I am,
Surrendering all gifts at Your Palace of Light.

GOLDEN TEMPLE *Amritsar, India*

WITH HUMILITY AND GRATITUDE
JAY PRAKASH SINGH, RABINDRA PAUL SINGH
JANICE SINGH, KANWAL PRAKASH SINGH
INDIANAPOLIS, INDIANA, U.S.A

Golden Temple, Amritsar, India - 1588

ਲਿ ਗੁਰੁ ਨਾਨਕੁ ਦੇਵ ॥

January 1988
K.P.Singh

THE ARTIST AT GOLDEN TEMPLE *Amritsar, India*

239

Kanwal Prakash Singh

The logo which appears on all Singh artwork is a composition of three letters-KPS-in Devanagri script. Hindi, the national language of India, is written in Devanagri script. The three stylized initials are written vertically and are enclosed in a square. The use of Devanagri reflects Mr. Singh's Indian background and interest in script as an element in design.

ACKNOWLEDGEMENTS

This book would not have been possible without the guidance and support of many talented people. Special thanks to my sons Rabindra Paul and Jay Prakash and my wife Janice for helping me with the myriad details that needed attention and for their generous contribution to the format and spirit of this endeavor.

My special gratitude to my parents and my family in India for their thoughtful prayers, inspiration, and boundless affection; their understanding and example guide my life, faith, and spirit. I remember with deep humility and gratitude the special gifts of many whose wisdom and encouragement enriched my thoughts and spirit.

I deeply appreciate the talents of Lloyd Brooks, Amy Royal, and staff in designing the book and the generous assistance and expertise of Midwest Graphics in faithfully scanning the intricate drawings and artwork for printing. Special thanks to Guild Press Emmis Publishing for this invitation and opportunity and an elegant presentation of my artwork and writings to the public.

A very special thank you to my friend U.S. Senator Richard Lugar for the distinct honor of writing a very thoughtful foreword to the book.

For comments and contact - Email: KP@kpsinghdesigns.com
Also visit: www.kpsinghdesigns.com